Outdoor Education
for the
Whole Child

Frederick A. Staley

Arizona State University

KENDALL/HUNT PUBLISHING COMPANY
2460 Kerper Boulevard, Dubuque, Iowa 52001

B   401993   01

Contents

Preface

This book is designed to provide guidance and ideas for the use of the outdoors by elementary school teachers to enhance development of the whole child. Outdoor education is not a separate discipline to be infused into the school curriculum. Rather, outdoor education is a method of utilizing the outdoors to enrich and enhance the child's life.

The title of the book emphasizes the Whole Child because there is no aspect of the child's intellectual, social, emotional, and physical development that cannot be enriched by teachers and the school's curriculum. *Outdoor Education for the Whole Child* provides both a rationale for the importance and use of the outdoors with children and with many practical suggestions and ideas for planning, managing, teaching, and monitoring the children's outdoor experiences.

The methodology and activity suggestions of this book pertain to all disciplines and thus could be used by any elementary school classroom teacher or as a supplement to any undergraduate or graduate methods course.

Special thanks is given to all the students and teachers who have reviewed and tried out the suggestions in this book and to James Huber, Jr. for permission to use many of the photographs in this book.

F.A. STALEY

Part One
Rationale and Methodology

Part One of this book provides a definition for outdoor education and a rationale for using the outdoors to enhance the development of the whole child. Useful suggestions are also given for planning, using resources, managing children, and for effectively teaching children in the outdoors.

Chapter 1

Nature of Outdoor Education

Introduction

The outdoors has long been a source of inspiration and stimulation for learning and creativity. In 400 B.C. Socrates is said to have utilized the outdoors as the primary teaching resource to employ his inquiry (Socratic) method of teaching. Through the ages parents and elders have taken their children outdoors to teach them how to hunt for food, how and where to grow crops, and how to survive by living one with nature. The outdoors has always been a living classroom!

As technology began to change the world, however, occupations became more specialized, people moved away from rural life into cities, and there were fewer opportunities for parents to teach their children the lessons of the land. Instead, schools were organized to provide formal education which emphasized the basics of survival in the ever increasing industrial and technological society.

With education in schools becoming more removed from the land the need for formal outdoor education arose. Present programs of outdoor education were derived from the school camping movement begun in the United States in the early 1940's. While school or resident camping still flourishes today as a viable educational experience for children, the concept of outdoor education has evolved since then to accommodate various other educational trends including:

1. The use of a variety of other outdoor resources such as the school site and urban environment to enrich the school's curriculum,
2. *Environmental education* which emphasizes a knowledge and concern for environmental quality,
3. *Energy education* which emphasizes the wise use of our dwindling energy resources,
4. *Adventure education* which provides youth with exciting outdoor encounters and challenges; and
5. *Experiential education* which emphasizes learning from one's total life experiences.

While these recent educational movements emphasize different approaches and have somewhat different goals, they are all part of what is broadly referred to as outdoor education in this book.

What Is Outdoor Education?

Outdoor education is education in the real world of the out-of-doors. It is an extension of the classroom and a means of enriching the total experiences for learning and living provided by the school. Outdoor education, as some have envisaged it, is not just science taught in the outdoors or field trips to the forest. Neither is outdoor education another subject to be added to the school curriculum.

Outdoor education is also an informal method of teaching and learning which offers opportunities for: (1) participating in direct laboratory experiences for the identification and resolution of real-life problems, (2) acquiring skills with which to enjoy a lifetime of creative, productive, and healthful living, (3) attaining concepts, insights, and appreciations about human and natural resources, and (4) bringing children back in touch with those aspects of living where their roots were once firmly established.

Probably the most comprehensive, yet simple definitions of outdoor education was formulated by one of the founders of Outdoor Education in America, the late Dr. Julian Smith, who defined outdoor education as "... *education in, for, and about the outdoors.*"[1]

Outdoor education *IN* the outdoors implies all the various outdoor resources teachers can use to enrich the learning and lives of children. Besides the school site, and residential camp settings there are limitless other resources that can be used to achieve a variety of outdoor education purposes. These include: school or home neighborhoods, gardens, farms, cemeteries, city parks, recreation areas, forests, ponds, lakes, streams, business and industrial establishments, municipal buildings and structures, transportation centers, museums, zoos, nature centers, arboretums, power stations, water purification plants, garbage dumps, state and national parks and monuments, game management areas, fish hatcheries, and historical sites.

Outdoor education *FOR* the outdoors embodies the knowledges, skills, and appreciations necessary for enjoying and participating in outdoor experiences and pursuits. *FOR* also implies having these experiences with consideration for the environment. Thus, both the individual and the environment are mutual beneficiaries of an outdoor activity. Teaching children the importance of not picking wild flowers during a nature walk in the woods is an example of combining a learning experience with the preservation of a delicate natural plant that would soon wilt and die if it were taken from the natural environment.

Education *ABOUT* the outdoors encompasses the learning of various concepts, relationships, and phenomenon in the natural and man-made environment. The outdoors does not have a subject matter structure like the areas of mathematics, reading, science, and social studies, thus, draws upon all subject matter areas for its structure.

The relationship between *education in, for, and about the outdoors* and the total elementary school curriculum is shown in Diagram 1.

Why Outdoor Education?

Justification for outdoor education experiences by the school is based on two basic premises:

1. *"That which can best be learned inside the classroom should be learned there. That which can be learned in the out-of-doors through direct experiences, dealing with native materials and life situations, should there be learned."*[2]
2. *Outdoor education experiences must contribute, in some way, to the achievement of the educational goals of the school and classroom.*

Thus, teachers must always be aware that the outdoors is being used appropriately and not as an excuse to take children outdoors. Taking children on a nature walk where a series of mini-lectures are given by the teacher on what the adult chooses to identify and discuss is an example of an activity that is probably more appropriate as an indoor slide projection presentation.

Teachers must also be aware of the goals for education and have a clear perception of how outdoor education can contribute to these goals. The following is a list of broad educational goals for which many parents and teachers agree upon as the basis for educating today's children for tomorrow's world. Also included are statements of how outdoor education experiences can contribute to each of these goals.

1. *To develop children's knowledge and appreciation of their environment and man's relationship to this environment.*

With generations of people drawn away from the land there is now an urgent need for education to bring children back in contact with the environment. The machine age, industrialization,

Diagram 1

Outdoor Education in the Curriculum

Outdoor Education

Is . . .

Education IN the Outdoors

Education FOR the Outdoors

Education ABOUT the Outdoors

Use of outdoor settings as laboratories for classroom related field experiences, study, observation and research. Settings include:

FOR implies two things:

1. The learning of skills for outdoor living, recreation and survival.
2. A moral approach to the outdoors. Both the learner and outdoors should become better because of the experience.

Learning through an activity approach using inquiry-discovery techniques about outdoor environmental areas such as the following lend themselves to this catagory.

School Site

School Neighborhood

Parks and Recreation
   Areas

Camps

Industrial Sites

Forests, Farms, Gardens

Museums, Zoos, Santuaries
   and Preserves

State and Federal Lands

Private Lands

Ponds, Lakes, Streams

Many kinds of attitudes and appreciations are tied in with this aspect as well. The whole area of "environmental education" and concerns for the future life on earth are good examples.

Plant Life

Animal Life

Ecology

Weather

Climate

Soil, Rocks, Minerals

Astronomy

Culture

Science and Math	Social Studies	Health, P.E., Recreation	Language Arts	Art Music Crafts	Industrial Arts Homemaking	Adult Education	Health, Safety Citizenship	Clubs, Clinic School Assemb. Special Activ.

The Curriculum

automation, computerization, specialization of vocation, and urbanization have all resulted in the separation of man from his natural environment. As a result, we've resorted to an artificial and restricted process of rearing our young. Most education in schools and homes has prohibited children learning one of the most vital relationships on earth: man to nature.

The world outside the home and classroom is aesthetically pleasing as well as full of environmental problems. Children need to be exposed to both beauty and the pollution. It is unfortunate that many programs in environmental education dwell only on the problems and destruction of the environment. While it is important for children to be sensitized to these problems, how they occur, and how they can be solved, we might better do this by first helping children appreciate the delicacies of the natural systems in the outdoor environment. Outdoor education experiences can allow children to observe first-hand the interrelationships between plants, animals, and the physical environment and observe the positive and negative effects man has on the delicate balances in nature.

2. *To develop children's understandings, skills and appreciations needed to mentally, emotionally, physically, socially, and spiritually lead productive, creative, and enjoyable lives.*

Our society has surrounded us with many conveniences such as fast food meals, instant world-wide communication, rapid transportation, and home entertainment via television, stereo, radio, and computer. While these have the potential to become useful tools of man, there is also the tendency for man to become tools of these devices. It is unfortunate that many adults have already allowed the pursuit of material possessions and the addiction of vicarious experiences to dominate their lifestyles and their values.

It is apparent that in order for today's children to lead productive and enjoyable lives in an ever changing world the educational system must be able to help children find appropriate avenues for coping with these changes. The adventure and outdoor pursuits aspects of outdoor education have as their basic tenents the development of children's skills of living in and enjoying the out-of-doors as well as the building of the confidence in one's self to attempt to use these skills.

Learning of such skills as archery, boating, orienteering (use of map and compass), fishing, and rock climbing can not only contribute to the growth and development of the individual child but provide him/her with life-long interests and hobbies.

3. *To develop children's skills and motivation to learn how to learn (i.e., how to find problems, solve problems, and make decisions).*

The world is changing so rapidly that it is impossible to prepare children for what life will be like when they are adults. What we can do is help motivate children to develop and utilize skills needed to deal with and understand change and how it occurs. Learning how to learn new things, to recognize problems, to gather information, to use available resources, and to solve problems is part of learning how to learn. As citizens in a democratic society children also need to learn how to weigh issues, understand alternatives, and make decisions with regard to such things as voting in elections, buying a home, choosing a career, and selecting a spouse.

The outdoor environment is full of real problems, many of which children can recognize, understand, and attempt to solve. Problems such as excessive litter on the playground or traffic congestion around the school can be studied, solutions offered, and remedy actions taken. Not only will children be contributing to the resolution of problems that are relevant and meaningful to their lives, but they will be learning the skills of how to learn which can be then used the rest of their lives.

4. *To develop children's ability to evaluate and improve their concepts of personal achievement and self-worth.*

The view a child has of him/her self and what he/she is capable of doing is a very powerful ingredient in learning. Self-image, for instance, determines the openness to learning; whether a child will even attempt to participate in a learning experience.

A child's self-concept is the child's inferences made about self on the basis of his/her experiences with other people and the environment. Because a child's self-concept can change and become more positive with successful experiences, it is important that teachers provide the right kinds of encounters with people and things as well as providing a supportive learning environment that will allow the child an opportunity to successfully evaluate and improve his/her self-concept.

Activities in the outdoors provide countless opportunities for children to encounter and work with people that cannot be found in the home or classroom. Outdoor activities also provide an alternative type of learning experience to indoor learning activities. Many children who are unsuccessful with rules, regulations, time schedules, and types of book learning of the indoor curriculum usually develop poor self-concepts. Participating in the more informal, active, and real world of the outdoors provides opportunities for these children to succeed and feel good about themselves in ways they are unable to indoors.

5. *To develop children's skills and understandings required to work and learn cooperatively with other individuals.*

Even a walk on a log can provide an adventure that may enhance the child's concept of self.

We do live in a highly cooperatively oriented society despite the fact that recent emphasis seems to be on the competitiveness of school and life. Cooperation is required in family living, most careers, athletic events, workings of the political system, and living with others in a community. Thus, children should be taught the skills and understandings needed to cooperate with others. Some of the important cooperative skills and understandings are: learning how to lead, learning how to follow, learning how to empathize with and recognize other's feelings, and learning how to treat others as human beings rather than as objects or tools.

Opportunities for children to work and learn together and thus learn the skills and understandings of cooperation are abundant in outdoor education. Experiences in social living such as planning activities and the acceptance of individual and group responsibilities for conducting activities can occur in the outdoors. First-hand experiences connected with group living related to menu planning, food preparation, care of facilities, and student government are especially evident in residential camping programs. Furthermore, the necessity to work through social problems which may arise in a twenty-four hour a day experience make the resident camp type of learning experience one that cannot be equaled in the classroom.

6. *To develop the creative potentials within each child.*

All children have the potential of creating something new and unique and thus contributing to their, and possibly other people's enjoyment of life. It is the job of the school to provide such a variety of learning experiences that each child will be able to discover and develop whatever creative capacities are present.

It is no accident that the inspiration for many creative works of art, poetry, music, and drama come from the out-of-doors. The mystique the outdoors has on us all is somewhat unexplainable. It does exist, however, as a powerful source and motivator for freeing children's inhibitions about writing, speaking, drawing, singing, etc., and outdoor education programs can capitalize on the mystique in ways that are often artificial when attempted indoors.

Observation. You'll notice in this list of broad educational goals there is no mention of learning the basic concepts and skills of computation and communication. This does not mean many parents and teachers do not think these are unimportant. On the contrary, the present concern with "Back to the Basics" attests to the fact that people do think basics are important. Basics are important, but only because they are the means through which the broader goals identified above can be achieved. Effective outdoor education programs contribute significantly to the development of basic skills. Working in the real world does provide the motivation to learn the basics of communicating and computation in order for children to express what has been observed and accomplished in the outdoors.

Conclusion

The scope of outdoor education has been presented in this chapter. Hopefully you'll begin to see the possibilities the outdoors has for enriching the goals and objectives you have for teaching and raising children in today's society. The remainder of this book provides some theoretical understandings needed to effectively meet the needs of children through outdoor experiences as well as providing a wealth of practical examples of how this theory can be carried out.

Notes

1. Julian W. Smith and others, *Outdoor Education* (Englewood Cliffs, N.J.: Prentice-Hall, 1963) p. 19.
2. L.B. Sharp, source unknown.

Chapter 2

The Whole Child

Introduction

"Outdoor education has moved into a decade bright with promise,"[1] according to one of the countries leading outdoor educators, Dr. George Donaldson. Current exploration of the hemispheric functions of the brain will surely help fulfill this promise by shedding more light than ever before on the validity of outdoor education experiences.

Briefly stated, the recent discoveries about how we think and learn suggest that the human brain has two distinct kinds of thinking capabilities: the intuitive and aesthetic, and the logical and rational. Knowledge of this can help explain that mystique the outdoors has had for helping children develop into healthy individuals capable of combining all parts of their being into an emotional, physical, social, and intellectual meld that defies trial, tribulations, and troubles.

While outdoor educators have long struggled to explain this mystique, most research attempting to justify outdoor education, like the focus of indoor education, was on a limited area of children's learning—that being on the analytical and rational thought processes. Such a peacemeal approach to the study of education defies the way all living creatures, especially humans, learn and develop.

Man's capacity to imagine, visualize, respond simultaneously to all sensory stimuli, and to use intuition to solve problems have all too rarely been considered or measured in education. Yet, as hemispheric research indicates, these abilities are of prime importance to the living of healthful, productive, and creative lives. Furthermore, this research also indicates that learning in math, science, reading, social studies, language arts, and the fine arts can be enhanced when consideration is given to both hemispheres of the brain in the learning process.

Hemispheric Brain Research

Although scientists have known for a long time that the human brain has two sides or hemispheres it was thought, until very recently, that the two sides mirrored each other in function, and in addition, in most people the left hemisphere was dominant. Now, massive evidence indicates something quite different. It has been established that the two hemispheres are responsible for quite different functions and capabilities. Yet, they do not work completely independently from one another but apparently communicate through a bundle of connecting nerves called the *corpus callosum*.

Studies done with epilepsy patients whose corpus callosums were surgically severed to reduce seizures and with normal subjects confirms a remarkable degree of differences between the functions of the two hemispheres. (Diagrams 1 and 2 provide examples of how some of this research was conducted.) We now know the left hemisphere is usually the site of logical and rational thought while the right hemisphere is usually the center of intuitive and aesthetic thought. Let us go into these in more detail.

Diagram 1

Experiments with Epileptic Patients[2]

Surgery had been conducted on the *corpus callosum* to isolate seizures so they would not transfer from one side of the brain to the other. While a seizure was going on in one side of the brain it was hoped the other side would take over control of the body. It worked, and the patients continued their lives with no apparent repercussions from the surgery.

These patients were later given several tasks which revealed how each hemisphere functioned without the opportunity for communication between the hemispheres. One such experiment was as follows: The phrase *key ring* was shown to the patients, set at the mid point of the visual field so that the first word, *key,* was seen only by the left eye (which is controlled by the right hemisphere) while the latter, *ring,* was relayed to the left hemisphere by the right eye. When asked to read the word they had seen, the subjects said "ring."

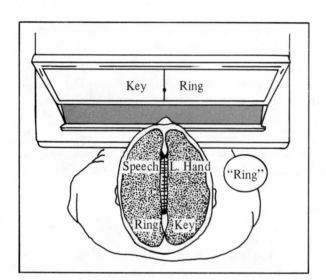 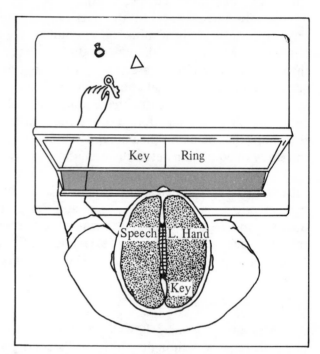

When asked to retrieve the object with their left hand (controlled by the right hemisphere) from a group of objects on the table, the subjects picked up the key, without realizing any contradiction in what they were doing.

In other words, with these patients, each hemisphere had its own inner visual world, cut off from the conscious awareness of the other. The left hemisphere responsible for the reading and verbal function and the right hemisphere responsible for the perceptual and tactile function.

Diagram 2

Experiments with Normal Subjects[3]

Normal subjects with no apparent brain damage were used in these experiments. Electroencephalograph electrodes were placed on the skull over both hemispheres of the brain. The electrodes detect brain wave activity in each hemisphere while the subjects are doing different tasks.

In one experiment right-handed subjects were asked to write a letter. The results indicated the left brain hemisphere was in charge and the right hemisphere "idled." It was thus inferred the left brain must control writing for right-handed subjects.

When the subjects were asked to arrange blocks into a pattern, the left half of the brain relaxed while the right half was active. Clearly, each side of the brain had worked out its own area of expertise, its own way of looking at things, its own way of processing information and gaining knowledge.

The left hemisphere, as can be seen in Diagram 3, for most individuals, is the site of logical, analytical, linear, and propositional thought. It controls such functions as talking, reading, writing, mathematical calculation, immediate verbal recall, time sense, order, and most functions that involve linguistic and numeric processes. In addition, the left hemisphere controls the right side of the body.

In the experiments described in Diagrams 1 and 2 the left brain controlled reading and writing because both tasks require an understanding of the rules of order and sequence. For example, to read or write the letters *C A T,* one has to be aware of these rules of sequence and order in order to communicate *cat* to someone. The letters *A C T* are the same but note how the sequence and order of reading and writing them can change the meaning.

The right hemisphere, differing but just as important, is the locus of intuition, imagination, fantasy, dreams, drawing, spatial perception, holistic understanding (a kind of I-suddenly-see-the-whole-thing-before-me thinking), perceptual insight, tactile sensations, musical ability, visualization and visual memory, and perhaps many of our emotions. The right hemisphere is virtually non-verbal and is the control of the left side of the body.

In the experiments described in Diagrams 1 and 2 the right side of the brain controlled tasks involving the visual perception of and manipulation of whole objects. Order sense and sequential abilities are not needed to recognize objects immediately and to arrange blocks into patterns because the right brain can deal with objects holistically. For example, a triangular shape is always triangular, no matter how it is turned. Thus $\triangle$, $\triangle$, $\triangledown$, and $\triangle$ are all symbols that are immediately recognizable as triangles. Changing the direction of them, unlike changing the order of letters in *C A T,* does not alter the meaning.

Many acts of creativity which require an individual to sense something tactilely, visually, spatially, or through dreams and fantasy and then express the results of this activity via some form of writing, art, music, or drama must utilize the functions of both hemispheres of the brain. Remember the right hemisphere is non-verbal and it must rely on the ability to communicate what it senses and thinks through the corpus callosum to the left side of the brain. Then, if it is desirable to express in some form what has been experienced, the left brain can assist. In reviewing the evolution of the human brain Sagan concluded by saying "I think the most significant creative activities of our or any other human culture—legal and ethical systems, art and music, science and technology—were made possible only through the collaborative work of the left and right cerebral hemispheres. These creative acts, even if engaged in rarely or only by a few, have changed us and the world. We might say that human culture is the function of the corpus callosum."[4]

Diagram 3

Resident Capabilities and Functions of Left and Right Hemispheres

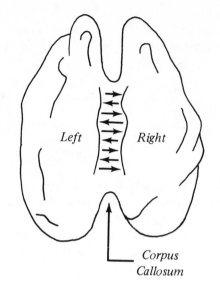

LEFT

Capabilities

—Linear-sequential thinking (one idea builds on another)

—Analytical-logical-rational thinking

—Deductive thinking

—Propositional thinking (if-then)

—Objective (correct proof)

RIGHT

Capabilities

—Simultaneous-holistic thinking (senses over-all patterns, relationships, and concepts at once)

—Intuitive-imaginative-metaphoric thinking

—Inductive thinking

—Appositional thinking (spatial forms and relationships)

—Subjective (feelings, values, emotions, dreams)

Corpus Callosum

Functions

—Controls right eye and right side of body

—Deals with details and separate parts

—Deals with significance of relationships across time

—Language and Logic (words are tools)

—Temporal

—Dominant control of skill hand and speech center

—Immediate Recall

—Reading, mathematics, writing, decoding speech skills

Functions

—Controls left eye and left side of body

—Deals with unity and total picture

—Deals with relationships perceived across space

—Does not understand language (visual/spatial abilities are tools)

—Present Centered

—Control of body awareness, body movement, body language, body in relation to environment

—Long term memory

—Imagery, fantasizing, dreaming, feelings

Notes:

1. The emerging picture of cerebral dominance is a complex one and the previous diagram is somewhat oversimplified. Obviously, the two hemispheres cannot work completely independently or no one would be able to carry out the simplest coordinated activity such as walking or speaking. When one side of the brain is damaged it is sometimes possible for the other side to learn to perform some of the functions of the damaged side.

2. The above function locations are true for about 90-95% of the right-handed people in the world. Eighty-five to 90% of the world is right handed. The above is only true for about 60-65% of the world's left handers. Functions are reversed for those whom it is not true.

3. Individuals differ greatly with regard to the above functions. Some have a preference for left brain functioning and may have superiority in the verbal area but not necessarily in the visual/spatial area. For others the opposite is true and many individuals are mixed or amidominant, having no favored side.

4. It is still uncertain what the connection is between handedness and the cerebral hemispheric functions. Some evidence suggests that left handers are more likely to have problems with such left hemisphere functions as reading, writing, speaking and arithmetic; and to be more adapt at such right-hemispheric functions as imagination, pattern recognition, and general creativity.[5]

Societies Discrimination of the Right Hemisphere

Recent findings regarding the importance of both hemispheres of the brain for learning and growing are surprising and significant when considering how the right hemisphere has been discriminated against by past and present societies.

Ancient customs subtly underlined these recent findings, for, in many primitive tribes left-handedness (controlled by the right side of the brain) was considered bad luck. The Bible repeatedly equated left handedness with evil while associating the right hand with truth and virtue. In the Moslem world the left hand has been considered unclean and is never offered in a social gesture.

Today we give a person a "left-handed complement" to imply something negative. We shake hands with the right hand, not the left. Honored guests set at the right side (controlled by the left hemisphere) of the host. Females stand on the left, the subordinate side, in the marriage ceremony. Meanings of the word "left" around the world also have negative connotations. For instance, note the following meanings for the word *left: gauche* in French also means awkward, *link* in German also means clumsy, *a zurdas* in Spanish also means wrong way, and *mancino* in Italian also means dishonest. Even our own English word, *left* comes from an Old English word, *lyth,* which meant worthless. Our words *sinister* and *dexterity* are derived from the Latin for left (sinister) and right (dexter) respectively.

Cameras and doors are right handed. So are scissors, can openers, rulers, power tools, egg beaters, pencil sharpeners, and gum wrapper tabs. Screws screw to the right. Irons iron to the right. Watches wind to the right. Guitars strum to the right. Telephones dial to the right. Even slot machines have the arm on the right. All these examples and more lend evidence to the value of *NOT* being left handed.

Similar kinds of discrimination against the right hemisphere have been carried out in our educational institutions as well. It was not too long ago that children were punished in school if they attempted to write left-handed. Even worse has been the squelching of children's right brain thinking powers. Rennels asked, "With Western man's primary institutional emphasis upon left cerebral functions, are educators overlooking a significant number of students who have highly developed right hemispheres?"[6] It could be that with too heavy an emphasis on the cognitive aspects of reasoning, logic, and objectivity, schools will systematically eliminate opportunities for children to develop visualization, imagination, and sensory/perceptual skills.

Many neurologists claim schools are discriminating against the right hemisphere because of the belief that man's technological development and survival have been contingent upon the left brain processes of scientific thought, i.e., development of verbal and numerical skills.[7] Thus, man's institutions have emphasized and nurtured the same mental processes that were responsible for his prior accomplishments. Unfortunately, all the right brain functions carried out by the scientists who created and tested theories and the workers who designed and built the technological world were overlooked.

Support is provided for the reasons given by many neurologists for the discrimination of right brain functions in schools when an analysis is made of the educational emphasis of cognitive development in the last twenty-five years. Such an emphasis was brought about because of the launch of Sputnik in 1957. Since then massive amounts of money have been provided by the Federal Government (NDEA and NSF) and foundations such as the Ford Foundation for Advancement in Education to support research and curriculum development projects aimed at developing children's logical, scientific, and objective approaches to learning in such subjects as science, mathematics, and social studies.

While this emphasis and approach to curriculum development and research was criticized for being the work of scholars and scientists rather than considering the ideas of teachers, and for stressing intellectual development at the expense of emotional and social development,[8] the movement continued. There was a host of other "left brain" reasons for its continuation, however. These included the influence and acceptance of Bloom's Taxonomy of cognitive learning tasks, literature on homogeneous grouping, competency based and programmed instruction, the use of operant conditioning to train the left brain, and the universal acceptance of Piaget's theories of cognitive, left brain development. This is not to say these left brain emphases have not been valid. Rather, it is to say these positions have focused only on children's left brain abilities and development. With the exception of work by such people as L. Kohlberg[9] on moral development there has been limited theory development or research on such right brain functions as dreams, fantasies, holistic thinking, intuition, and emotions.

Another factor that has perpetuated the unbalanced emphasis on the left brain functions in schools has been because the test of left brain functions, i.e., acquisition of number facts and reading skills, has been easier than measuring right brain functions such as spontaneity, creativity, and intuition. While the left brain functions are certainly important to the successful management of our lives, there is more to living and thinking than counting and recognizing words. Says Robert Ornstein, "The capacity to produce a striking synthesis, to create anew, rarely falls within the multiple choices offered on standard tests. Indeed, how could such creation be programmed? It is not the fault of the tests so much as it is the assumptions of the questioners, oriented as they have been to the common denominator, the 'basics' of verbal analysis and arithmetic. What has been considered 'basic' in our schooling is but a small segment of our capacity."[10] Recent concerns with "Back to the Basics" could contribute even further to an education that is geared for only one half of the child's mind.

Implications of Split Brain Research for Education

Outdoor educators, with their historical concern for the whole child living in consonance with nature, join researchers and other educators in examining the educational implications of this hemispheric research. Three significant implications are as follows:

1. *An examination of the testing and teaching practices of children who are labeled or become learning disabled must take on new perspectives.* Recent research on hemispheric functions has already provided useful information in identifying and remediating children with learning disabilities. However, knowledge of the discrimination against right brain functions in our educational institutions in the last twenty-five years raises two serious questions:

   A. How many children are incorrectly labeled as deviant because they daydream, wiggle, talk, examine their surroundings (all right brain actions), and generally seem to get into trouble because they don't sit quietly and listen (left brain actions) in the classroom?

   B. Are perhaps many of the children who are classified as deviant, learning disabled, dyslexic, hyperkenetic, and emotionally disturbed products of too early and too extensive an emphasis on left brain (back to the basics) learning strategies?

2. *Education must again become child centered.* That is, each individual child with two hemispheres of the brain and body must be considered when determining appropriate learning experiences and teaching methodologies. It is clear that the whole child has been neglected in the last twenty-five years of educational practice. This has not always been the case, however, because the history of education is replete with philosophies and practices that emphasized whole child-whole brain development. Some of these practices and approaches are briefly described below.

   A. Pestalozzi's *naturalistic theory* of education (1764–1827) as a process of generalizing upon a number of sensory experiences is representative of left and right brain learning experiences. Pestalozzi emphasized a method of teaching which started from children's interests and then used objects, field trips, shop work, and inductive lessons to proceed from the concrete to the abstract.

B. The creator of the *kindergarten,* or "garden of children," Frobel (1782–1852), continued the Pestalozzian tradition. Kindergarten was to be a place where the use of special materials would help children's innate, splendid natures unfold as flowers unfold. Without question, his emphasis upon allowing children of four and five to learn through play and fantasy was an insight of high order. Frobel also believed there was something magical about the effect handling objects had on the mind and spirit of children. Were these not right brain approaches to learning that were not magical after all?

C. It also appears the recent hemispheric research is a reaffirmation of John Dewey and the whole *progressive education-activity curriculum* movement of the early twentieth century. In 1899 Dewey indicated that the educational center of gravity had too long been ". . . in the teacher, the textbook, anywhere and everywhere you please, except in the immediate instincts and activities of the child himself."[11] Later, in 1921, Bosner wrote of progressive education, "The curriculum should provide for all phases of behavior: acting, thinking, and feeling. In the conduct of life, thinking and feeling are of quite as much importance as is acting in a motor sense."[12] In a discussion of the activity program in 1937 Melvin condemned traditional education by saying, "Modern education with its science and its philosophy and its incessant involvement with psychology and statistics has forgotten children. It has lost the dynamic conception of childhood. It has examined the most intricate processes of learning each in isolation. In these forests of psychology we have lost sight of the tree itself. . . . We have remembered our 'subject' of education, but we have forgotten its object—the whole human child."[13] Could this not also be said of the unbalanced left brain approach to educating children in our schools in the last twenty-five years?

3. *Present attempts to provide more humanistic education of children must be continued.* Humanism operates on the basic theory that the individual has "internal" components which affect perceptions, feelings, values, beliefs, attitudes, motivations, as well as individual's cognitions and actions.[14] Hemispheric research may provide the key to understanding the nature of these "internal" components, i.e., the functions of the right and left brain.

The implications cited above all reflect the importance of considering what is basic about the learning and growth of each individual child. It now seems clear the real basics of education should emphasize not only the left brain functions of reading, writing, and arithmetic and the right brain functions of feeling, imagining, and intuition but the union of left and right brain functioning which is the essence of creativity. As was also indicated, the provision for children to learn by using both hemispheres is not really a new idea but in the last twenty-five years the educational climate has made this difficult to achieve. Outdoor education, a product of progressive-activity education, is certainly in a place to revitalize education of the whole child.

Outdoor Education for the Whole Child

If outdoor education is to have a place in contributing to the education of the whole child then the following question must be answered: "How can outdoor education help children develop both hemispheres of their brains in ways that will allow them to become healthy, creative, and productive individuals?"

Outdoor education has always been unique in being able to meet the needs of the whole child. It is hard to be cognitive, numerical, and objective when facing a gorgeous butterfly, a waterfall, a ponderosa pine, or a full moon. The observing of rain, conducting a bird count, measuring tree rings, and the timing of the growth of a century plant cannot be done with only one side of the brain. The corpus callosum is busy!

But, let us be specific about how outdoor education can contribute to the development of the whole child.

1. By providing resources that emphasize learning by doing (right brain) as well as thinking about what is being done (left brain). Education in the outdoors not only lends itself, but, indeed, impells learners to use the outdoors as a living laboratory full of concrete objects and ideas to observe, manipulate, fantasize about, analyze, measure, and record.

When children investigate soil with their hands, they have the opportunity to fantasize as well as analyze.

2. By employing an informal methodology that encourages children to select learning strategies (left, right, or mixed) that suit their styles of dealing with the environment and environmental relationships. The outdoor environment often encourages the use of art, drama, fantasy trips, and music (right brain), and graphs, charts, reading, writing, discussions (left brain), poetry, stories, and music writing (left and right brain). Furthermore, outdoor learning provides an escape from the stereotypes of bells, timetables, and desks of the classroom.

3. By providing real life situations and problems with which children can have problem finding (right brain) and problem solving (left brain) learning experiences that are relevant and meaningful to their lives.

4. By providing an opportunity for children to observe and accomplish things not possible in the classroom such as rock climbing, cave crawling, over-night camping, hiking, insect collecting, and star gazing. Such activities provide the right brain with the necessary stimulus to

activate the left brain to think about the significance of such experiences for the child's life and education.

5. By providing a world as a classroom that is whole and unsegmented by content disciplines such as math, science and social studies. There are no artificial boundries such as might be found in textbooks. Thus, any topic or theme selected from the environment has the potential of providing integrated, whole, left and right brain learning experiences.

6. By providing unique opportunities for teachers and children to get to know one another's needs, interests, and life styles. This will eventually build the kind of rapport, respect, and trust needed for the teacher or children to feel safe to pursue right or left brain approaches to teaching and learning.

The best way to show how outdoor education experiences can effectively contribute to the education of the whole child is through a specific example. The following is a description of one activity along with an analysis of how the different steps in that activity help contribute to the left and right brain functions of the child.

Example of How an Outdoor Education Activity Enhances the Whole Child

Activity: Create an Animal[15]

Group: Classroom or Family Group with Children ages 8–12

Time of Year: Spring, Summer, Fall

Location: Anywhere in the Outdoors

Materials: Any assortment of construction materials (colored paper, water paint, glue, clay), junk (toothpicks, nuts and bolts, buttons scraps of cloth, etc.), and perhaps potatoes.

Lesson Overview: This activity provides children with a concrete experience with the concept of protective coloration in animals. Protective coloration is important to the survival of animals and insects because the ability to blend with the environment enables creatures to hide from enemies as well as become more effective hunters for animals and insects they eat. This activity provides an opportunity for children to learn about protective coloration by actually creating and finding a make believe animal that blends into a specific environmental location.

Procedure:

1. Take the children to a specified location within the outdoor environment (could be along a hedge row or next to the school building, or under a tree in a park or camp ground) and ask them to observe the area, noting the colors, shapes and textures of plants, ground material, and non-living things such as rocks and soil. Then ask them to think about and identify various places in this environment where animals or insects might be found (in shrubs, on leaves, on the ground, on trunks of trees, etc.).

2. Ask the children to think about a make believe, first size animal that could live in this environment in such a way that it would not easily be seen by other animals or people. Have them close their eyes and imagine how big the animal might be, how it will be able to move to escape enemies or to catch food, how it will sense (see, hear, touch, smell) its environment, how it will eat its food, and what color, shape, and texture it will have to be to help it blend in with the environment.

3. Take the children back indoors where they use the pile of collected materials to construct their make believe animal as close to how they imagined it with the materials available. The potatoes could be used for the body of their animal.

The creation of a make-believe animal helps combine left and right brain functions.

If there are several children doing this activity at the same time, they can work in teams of two, three, or four to build one animal that represents their combined fantasies.

4. Once they complete their make believe animal they take it back, individually, to the specified location and place it in the environment. The animal should not be buried or covered with anything, rather, placed in the open. The child then returns to the classroom.

5. When all the animals are in place the whole group returns to the specified areas to search for the hidden animals. As they are found they are placed on the ground according to the order they were found.

6. Once all are found a discussion can be held (either outdoors or indoors) about why it was easy or hard to find some of the animals. The leader can point out at this time that the ability to be hidden in an environment because an animal looks very much like its surroundings is called *protective coloration*. Each child should also have a chance to describe their animal by giving its name and by telling how it functions (eats, moves, senses its environment, and is protected by its coloration and structure).

7. When complete the children can then return to the classroom for a followup activity that will help fix the understanding of the concept. Any of the following activities could be done:

   A   Make a display of the created animals which includes a written description of each animal and its protective coloration.

   B.   Write a creative story about an exciting adventure their created animal has had that involves its protective coloration.

    C.   Make a chart which identifies the order these animals were found with a brief explanation of why each was found when it was.

    D.   Find pictures of organisms or view films of animals that show how their protective coloration helps them.

    E.   Take a field trip to the same general area and see if animals and insects can be found that are actually blending in with their environment.

Discussion and Analysis: Once the children have conducted this type of activity it has been found they not only can verbalize and explain the significance of the concept of protective coloration, but can create and find other examples of the idea in the real world outdoors. It is also amazing how much more observant children become on walks in the outdoors after doing this kind of activity because they know many animals and insects may be camouflaged because of their coloration and structure.

How can learning of a concept such as protective coloration be so meaningful and lasting for children? The answer is because the whole child was involved in the learning process. Look back over the procedures to see where left and right brain functions were encouraged.

In step 1 the learning was begun with a concrete experience with the concept, not with an adult attempting to verbalize the concept for the children; this didn't occur until step 6. Instead, children were encouraged to observe the total environment and find places where animals and insects might live. By providing the children the opportunity to view the total environment, to view the concept in real life, the child was forced to use the right hemisphere of the brain in a holistic manner. Information gathered was then used by the left hemisphere to analyze where animals or insects might be found.

In step 2 a type of fantasy trip was utilized to allow the children to activate the right side of the brain to mentally create an idea of what an animal might look like that could live in the environment observed.

This made it quite easy for the child to translate the fantasy into a creation of art in step 3. The art creation was a result of right brain images started outdoors and the left hemisphere thinking about how the images could be transposed with the pieces of junk and potatoes into an animal. This was a good example of creativity being the effective combination of right and left brain functions. If the opportunity was provided for children to work together in creating an animal, then group cooperative skills could also have been developed.

In step 4 the significant learning aspect was that the child had to utilize the concept of protective coloration, even though they didn't have a label for it yet to place their invented animal appropriately in the environment. Again, the child was forced to consider the total environment which stimulated right brain functions. The analysis of specific aspects of the environment, i.e., colors, shapes, textures, required left brain functions. Another point worth making was that the child again was physically involved with materials and the environment.

In step 5 the children were involved again in carefully observing the environment, which capitalized on both right and left brain functions, in order to search for other hidden animals.

In step 6 a discussion lead by the adult utilized left brain functions because children were involved primarily in listening and talking while analyzing the results of the animal hunt. In this step children were allowed to think about (left brain) what they had done (right brain) which was an attempt to combine functions of both hemispheres of the brain.

In the final step of the procedure children were provided many opportunities to extend their learning. Note that some of the activities were primarily left brain (writing descriptions and making charts), some were primarily right brain (making a display and creative writing), and some combined both (viewing films and field trip). If children are given a choice of which activity to do, it is very likely they will select a type of activity that matches their hemispheric preference.

It should also be noted in step 7 that, although this activity was primarily science oriented, the options for extending the idea utilized creative writing, descriptive writing, reading and mathematics (making a chart). This is typical of many of the activities presented in this book because, as noted previously, outdoor education is interdisciplinary in nature.

Conclusion

It seems clear that the brain does have different functions and that learning in the outdoors does provide the necessary ingredients for stimulating both hemispheres of the brain. The previously undefined mystique of the outdoors may be its appeal to the right hemisphere of the brain. The outdoors, after all is holistic; communicating simultaneously with audible and nonaudible messages to all the senses. Further research should be conducted, however, on the effects of outdoor education experiences on children's development of intuition, imagination, inductive thinking, and feelings, emotions, values, and dreams before a definite link can be made between outdoor education and the right hemisphere of the brain.

Notes

1. George and Alan Donaldson, "Outdoor Education: Its Promising Future," *Journal of Health, Physical Education and Recreation,* April, 1972, page 23.
2. Wayne Sage, "The Split Brain Lab," *Human Behavior,* June, 1976, page 26.
3. Edwin Kiester Jr., and David W. Cudhea, "Robert Ornstein: A Mind for Metaphore," *Human Behavior,* June, 1976, page 17.
4. Carl Sagan, *The Dragons of Eden.* (New York: Ballentine Books, 1977), page 695.
5. *Ibid.,* page 188.
6. Max R. Rennels, "Cerebral Symmentry: An Urgent Concern for Education," *Phi Delta Kappan,* March, 1976, page 472.
7. *Ibid.,* page 471.
8. J. Murray Lee, *Foundations of Elementary Education.* (Boston: Allyn and Bacon, 1969), pages 76–77.
9. Lawrence Kohlberg and C. Gilligan, "The Adolescent as a Philosopher: The Discovery of the Self in a Postconventional World," *Daedalus,* 1971, pages 1051–1068.
10. Robert Ornstein, "Newsletter of the Institute for the Study of Human Knowledge," No Date.
11. John Dewey, *The School and and Society.* (Chicago, 1899), page 51.
12. Frederick Gordon Bosner, *The Elementary School Curriculum.* (New York: The Macmillan Co., 1921), page 22.
13. A. Gordon Melvin, *The Activity Program.* (New York: John Day, 1937), page 7.
14. David H. Ost, "Humanism, Science and Education," Chapter 7 of 1975 AETS Yearbook, *Science Teacher Education 1974: Issues and Positions.* (Columbus, Ohio: ERIC Center, Ohio State University, October, 1974.)
15. Derived from an *Outdoor Biology Instructional Strategies* activity called "Invent an Animal," *OBIS.* Lawrence Hall of Science, University of California, Berkeley, California.

Chapter 3

Thematic Unit Approach to Planning Integrated Outdoor Education Experiences

Introduction

The process described below is referred to as a *Thematic Approach* because it involves the identification and use of a central theme or topic as the focus for planning a unit of instruction. Organizing and planning units around themes provides many opportunities to integrate disciplines, thus is consistent with the interdisciplinary nature of outdoor education. Such an approach also provides opportunities to incorporate left and right brain functions and provide for large group, small group, and individual learning.

There are four possible theme categories for organizing a unit. Each is a slightly different basis for unifying the various disciplines. The four theme categories are as follows:

Concept Themes. Units organized around broad concepts are designed to provide children with the mental structures required to understand and describe the world around them. Some examples of broad generalizing ideas or concepts are change, interaction, energy cycle, death, birth, and system. Note, these usually can be designated by a single word.

Process Themes. Process themes are intended to give units a focus on methods of solving problems and making decisions. Both left and right brain processes can be used. Examples are communicating, guessing, fantasizing, and observing. Process skills are also important to effective functioning within other categories, however, they are the primary focus of units only within this category.

Persistent Problem Themes. Persistent problem themes allow children not only to understand and explain possible causes for problems that are persistent in their lives, but also enable children to apply what they know, particularly processes and concepts, to possible solutions to these problems. Examples that might be relevant concerns of some children are the energy shortage, traffic congestion around the school, and litter on the playground.

Natural or Man Made Phenomenon Themes. Units based on phenomenon will enable children through real and direct experiences to understand and describe the world around them. As with the previous category, there is no finite list of phenomenon that might be used with various ages of children. Possible examples are the desert, school site, park, or city. Actually, almost any natural or man made phenomenon, event, place, or structure will serve satisfactorily as a theme as long as it is derived from the realm of real and direct experiences of the child.

While thematic topics could be carefully selected by the teacher to meet preconceived needs, ideas, and objectives, they also could be generated spontaneously from the occurrence of a current event, happening, child's question, child's discovery, or child's problem. A few points worth making in this regard are that:

1. Any idea or theme that comes from the child has the built-in advantage of being relevant and meaningful to the child. Motivation for investigating and doing activities involving such a theme will probably be higher than a theme determined by a teacher.

2. Although activities and units within one theme will relate in many ways to other themes and categories, experience has shown that only one theme and category should be used as the organizer for a unit. This makes it easier to write unit goals that are focused toward the direction of the theme category.

3. Not all the activities developed that relate to an outdoor education theme need be done in the outdoors. For example, while a theme topic such as "Flying Things" lends itself to many direct experiences outdoors, there are perhaps many activities that could more appropriately be done indoors on this theme.

Developing a Thematic Unit

There is no rigid sequence for developing and planning a thematic unit, thus the following steps are suggestive rather than prescriptive. The sequence which follows, however, has been derived from an approach which has been generalized from several years of experience by teachers.[1] Along with a description and rational for each step an example is also provided for the development of a unit on "Flying Things."

Step 1. Select an appropriate theme and invent an appropriate title for the unit.

To be appropriate the theme and title should have the potential of integrating disciplines, providing concrete learning experiences, motivating students, contributing to the overall goals and objectives of the school system, and be within the child's ability range. It is also advisable not to pick a theme that is so broad and all encompassing that it is likely to be used by other teachers in later grades.

While it makes little difference what theme category the theme is in, it is probably desirable to have a year round program that represents a balance of themes from all four categories.

> Example: *Theme*
>
> Flying Things
>
> *Theme Category:* Natural and Man Made Phenomenon
> *Theme Title:* "Up, Up, and Away"
> *Grade Level:* Third Grade

Step 2. Develop a Rationale for the unit.

This is a statement of the reasons for the units' importance. It should be addressed to students and teachers alike. Once a unit gets under way or once a unit is retaught a second time, the written rationale helps to avoid the problem of forgetting the original reasons for justifying a particular unit.

> *Example: Rationale*

Many children are fascinated by flying things. Birds, butterflys, jet travel, space explorations, and satellites are already part of their everyday lives even before school. Children can further refine their understandings of both natural and man-made flights with a wide variety of experiences with flight and flying things. Such a unit also has the potential of helping children develop problem solving skills associated with conducting experiments dealing with such concepts as variables, gravity, and propulsion. Topics leading to understandings and appreciations of the history of flight are also related. Associated with man's attempts to adapt to non-terrestrial environments are also topics related to plant and animal adaptions for flight.

A unit on "Flying Things" has much imaginative appeal as well and there is the potential for conducting creative work through words, music, craft, and movement.

"Up, Up, and Away." The observation of a hot air balloon near school may be the prime motivation to study flying things.

Step 3. Decide on the length of the unit.

Deciding a length at this time provides a tentative guideline for the extent of planning required. With further planning it may be determined the unit should be longer or shorter. Even after instruction of the unit begins the time limit should remain flexible to allow for the fact that interest may wane or continue to be too high to cease the unit.

Time limits also depend in part on the age group with which the unit will be used and whether the unit represents the integration of several disciplines. If the unit truly integrates several disciplines more time per day and per week can be devoted to theme work, thus lessening the total time for the unit.

Example: Projected Length

Three weeks with 1 1/2–2 hours per day, four days a week.

Step 4. Produce unit goals.

These should be the broad student outcomes which indicate what the children will learn, *not* just what is to be done in the unit. The goals should be important for children, relate to the over-all curriculum goals, and represent a variety of knowledge, attitude, and skill outcomes.

Example: Unit goals

A. The children will have a greater understanding of natural and man-made flying things and the similarities and differences between them.
B. The children will further refine problem solving skills of identifying a problem, collecting data, determining alternative solutions, acting on an acceptable solution, and evaluating the results of the action.
C. Children will be able to discuss the history of man's flight, the present status of flight, and the future of flight.
D. Children will be able to utilize a variety of modes of expression to indicate their newly acquired understandings, skills, and appreciations.

Step 5. Brainstorm all possible sub-themes, topics, or activities that relate to this main theme.

Brainstorming is a process of generating ideas and fifty ideas in five minutes is not unusual for a group if certain rules are followed.

The originator of brainstorming, Alex Osborn, suggested the following requirements for all participating in the brainstorming process.[2] Anyone can learn to apply them to thematic unit planning if these rules are followed:

A. Defer judgement. Analysis and criticism comes later.
b. Free-wheel. Hang loose, let the right brain function. Think of the unusual, unique, or bizzare. Don't worry about order and sequence.
C. Tag on. Don't wait for an idea. Make another one out of the last one given by changing it in some way.
D. Quantity is wanted. Don't hold back for a minute.
E. Be child like in your thinking. How would children in your class respond in the same process to this theme topic? Better yet, allow the children to participate with you in the brainstorming. This will give you clues to the children's background with the theme as well as determine children's interest.

Your ability to utilize the brainstorming process will not only depend on your knowledge and experience of what has or could be done with the theme topic, but your ability to participate in the free-wheeling required of the brainstorming process itself. Descriptions of available materials, resources, and activities such as those described in this book will help provide the necessary knowledge and experience. You may need practice, however, in releasing your mind to brainstorm. After all, brainstorming is primarily a right brain activity and many adults have been so indoctrinated in sequential and logical thinking processes that it is sometimes difficult to free the right side of the brain to think non-sequentially and non-logically. If you, or you and the children have great difficulty coming up with sub-themes, ideas, or activities this could either mean that (1) your theme is not lively enough or appropriate for the children or (2) you are not following the rules of brainstorming.

Here is an example of how to proceed with this phase of the thematic unit planning process:

A. Write a theme or topic in the center of a blank piece of paper. See the example which follows.

B. Begin to let the ideas this theme brings to mind flow and add these anywhere on the sheet. Numbers in the following example are placed next to each idea only to indicate the brainstorming sequence used by one person. No two diagrams will ever look alike because a theme and sub-themes will call to mind different things for different people. Arrows indicate that one idea leads to another.

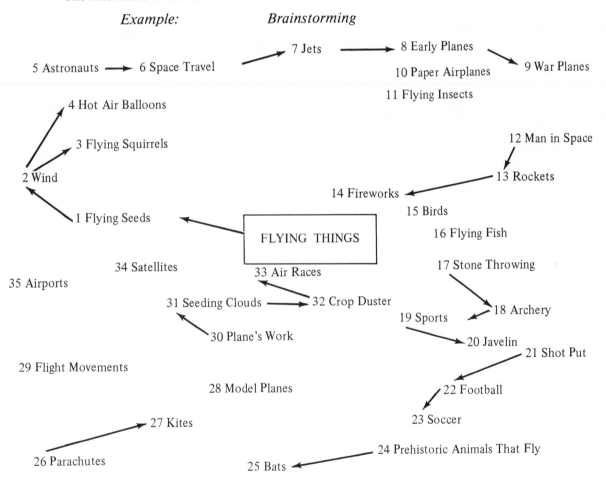

Example: *Brainstorming*

Step 6. Once you've brainstormed all the possibilities, go back over the diagram and reorganize the ideas you have onto a new sheet.

This time you can be concerned with order and sequence. Put those ideas, activities, or sub-themes together that have something in common, from your point of view. Notice in the reorganized diagram that follows that arrows are used to show how various sub-themes flow from the central theme and how additional ideas flow from the sub-themes. This new arrangement may now suggest further ideas that were overlooked in the first brainstorming session. If so, add these to the new diagram. The result is called a *Flow Diagram* or *Idea Web* because of the way some of the sub-themes flow and mesh together.

Example: *Revised Brainstorming*

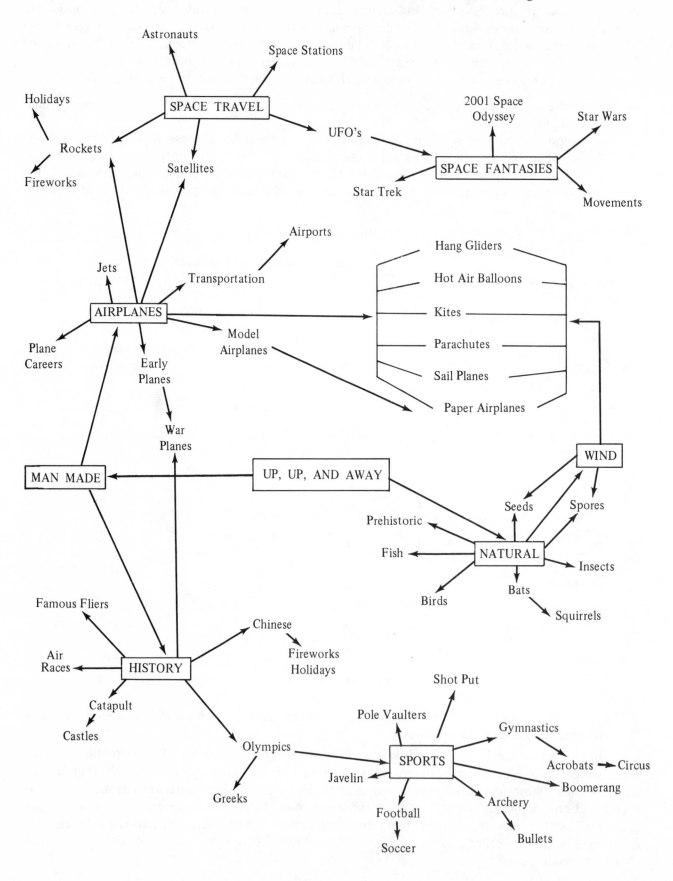

Step 7. *Isolate Possible New Themes.*

At this point some of the sub-themes may appear to have the potential of becoming themes on their own. These should be placed toward the exterior of the page to give room for additional brainstorming. The brainstorming involving these sub-themes could then be saved for later use if it appears the unit, as it is, will be too unwieldy to include them.

Example: Isolated themes

In the previous flow diagram the sub-topics Wind, Circus, Castles, Sports, and Olympics are so broad in scope they could become themes on their own.

Step 8. *Review and Analyze the Diagram.*

Assuming you have the desire to create an interdisciplinary unit, one that provides experiences that utilize the outdoors, and one that is appropriate for both hemispheres of the brain, examine the diagram again to answer the following questions:

"Where is the science in the diagram?"
"Where are the social studies?"
"Where is the math?"
"Where is the language arts?"
"Where is the art, music, drama, physical education?"
"Where is the reading?"
"How could the school site contribute?"
"How could other available resources be used?"
"Which of the activities are predominately right brain?"
"Which are predominately left brain?"

Example: Diagram Analysis

Where is the Science?

airplanes +
rockets
space travel
seeds +
animals +
fireworks
kites +

Where is the Social Studies?

history of flying
famous fliers
chinese-kits, fireworks
olympics—Greece
holidays—fireworks
Australia—Boomerang +

Where is the Reading?

trade books on topics
stories about
   topics
   biographies

Where is the Math?

estimating, measuring
   height, distance of model
   rocket +
timing speed +
volumn and temperature of
   hot air balloons +
symmetry in flight
   objects +
graphing results
counting birds +

Where is the Art?
kite making +, #
model planes +
hot air balloons +
mobiles +, #

Where is the Music
Sounds of flying things #
"Those Magnificent men in
   flying machines" #
"Yellow bird" #

Where is the Language Arts?
poems #
creative writing #
diaries
making books

Where is the P.E.?
movements +, #
sports +, #

Where is the Drama?
movements +, #
history plays

+ = school site or outdoors

= right brain activity

Step 9. Examine the revised diagram again to determine those sub-topics or activities that you would like to include in your unit.

Not everything will fit for a variety of reasons. Again, here are some things to consider in selecting the topics and activities to use:

A. Do the topics or activities have the potential of contributing to the unit goals?

B. Will the ideas or activities be interesting for the children? Are they real and meaningful to their lives? Are they within their realm of experience?

C. Are the activities or ideas appropriate for the child's intellectual, social, physical, and emotional abilities? All children need to learn by active involvement but the following general guidelines provide additional information about the kind of involvement appropriate for different ages of children:

   1. Children ages 1–7 should utilize their senses as the means to find out what is in the outdoors. Focus should be on such aspects as likenesses and differences and observation skills when starting an activity.

   2. Children ages 7–10 can extend observations to include making critical comparisons and simple measurements. It is also at this age that children become interested in collecting things.

   3. Children ages 11–13 are able to make comparative measurements, conduct sustained experiments, and use statistical procedures for calculating results of experiments.

D. Are many of the topics or activities do-able? That is, do many of them involve activity, not just reading about doing things or listening to others tell about doing things?

E. Are a mix of disciplines represented? Is there a balance of left and right brain activities? If you have a large group of children, are some of the activities appropriate for large groups? Are there some activities for small groups and individuals?

F. Are the topics and activities feasible? If you have sub-themes identified, will you be able to find activities for children to do to investigate these sub-themes, or will you have to invent your own activities? What resources do you have available to help you suggest possible activities? Also, are the activities you select within your constraints of time, materials, and money?

Example: Sub-themes to include/exclude

As you can see from the previous example, ideas for activities are beginning to emerge. For example, two songs were already thought of that relate to flight, and the idea of estimating height distances of model rockets came up after the brainstorming when the question "Where is the mathematics?" was asked.

Responses to questions A through F indicate that sub-themes are appropriate, activities well balanced, and there are possibilities for many doable experiences.

Step 10. Find or create activities to match sub-themes.

This is perhaps the most difficult and time consuming step in the entire process because the jump from a possible sub-theme to an activity involving that theme is not always easy. Your previous experiences doing activities that relate to the theme, knowledge of idea resources (like those described in Chapter 4, knowledge of ideas that could be found in available science, social studies, math, and language arts text books, knowledge of stories, poems, and songs in reading series and music books, and your imagination are important prerequisites to generating appropriate activities.

As you begin looking through resources for ideas to suit your theme and sub-themes chances are excellent you'll come across additional ideas you had not thought of in your brainstorming. If these ideas suit you and the children's needs, add them to your flow diagram.

Example: Resource the unit

Room does not permit inclusion of all the resources that could be used containing ideas relating to "Up, Up, and Away."

Step 11. Narrow and select activities to include in the unit.

Time for brainstorming is over. Decisions must now be made. Which of the possible sub-topics and activities should be included and which should be excluded from the unit? Criteria for making these decisions have already been identified in Steps 1, 3, 4, 8, and 9.

Based on your selections you should now have a better idea of the scope of the unit and you may want to readjust the time limit and/or the goals of the unit.

Example: Narrow Selections

The selections made are outlined in the example of the next step. Because the planning to this point, however, has revealed more possibilities than thought at the outset, the time limit of the unit has been increased to five weeks.

Step 12. Sequence and Outline the Unit.

One model[3] for unit outlines consists of three types of lessons:

A. *Introductory*—those designed to introduce children to the entire unit and the possible sub-themes, activities, and projects that can be experienced.
B. *Alternative*—all the possible sub-themes, activities, projects children can choose from in experiencing the theme and in achieving the goals of the unit. These are called alternative because it is assumed not every child will do every activity. Rather children will be able to choose from the available alternatives.
C. *Generalizing*—those activities designed to be used to provide a conclusion to the whole unit.

In attempting to sequence and outline the unit, those activities that would serve well as Introductory and Generalizing lessons should be determined first. Sequencing of the alternative activities should remain somewhat flexible; left to the interests of the children that emerge after the Introductory experiences.

As part of this step a chart outlining the essential features of each lesson should be constructed. This provides a "look at a glance" of the total unit which is useful for evaluating the balance of the entire unit in terms of the various features of the unit. These features which should be included are shown in the following example.

"Up, Up, and Away"
Unit Outline*

Sub-theme	Activity	Goal #	Size Group	Learning Model	Time	Disciplines	Brain Hemisphere	Scouce
Introductory Activities								
1. Natural	Things that fly on school site	1	Large/small	Fieldtrip	1 hr.	Science	L/R	Original
2. History	"History of flight"	3	Large	Movie	1/2 hr.	Soc. St.	L	McGraw Hill film
3. Balloons	Balloon messages	1, 2, 4	Small	Constructing	2 hrs.	Sci/L.A.	L/R	Original
4. Paper Airplanes	Making and testing	2	Small	Experiment	2 hrs.	Science	L/R	*SCIS* Energy resources
5. Flying things	Brainstorming	1-4	Large	Discussion	1 hr.	All	L/R	Original
Alternative Activities								
1. Birds	Visit an aviary	1	Large	Field Trip	1/2 day	Science	L	Original
2. Birds	"Bird Flight"	1	Small	Movie	1/2 hr.	Science	L	McGraw Hill film
3. Birds	Bird count on school site	1	Small	Fieldtrip	1 hr.	Science/Math	L	Sci 5-13
4. Birds	Music about birds	1 and 4	Small	Listening	1 hr.	Music	L/R	Original
5. Airport	Visit an airport	1	Large	Fieldtrip	1/2 day	Sci/Soc. St/Math	L	Original
6. Transportation	Plan a trip Send for info	1, 2, 4	Small/indivi.	Interview/reading writing	1 1/2 hr.	L.A./Math	L	Original
7. Airport	Build a model airport—past present, future	4	Indiv/small	Construction	1/2 day	Sci/Soc. St/L.A./Math	L/R	Sci 5-13

*Explanations of the various features of this chart are given in the next step.

Sub-theme	Activity	Goal #	Size Group	Learning Model	Time	Disciplines	Brain Hemisphere	Source
8. Insects	Wings, how, where distance of flight symetry	1	Small/indiv.	Experiment	1 hr.	Sci/Math	L	Sci 5-13
9. Hot air balloons	Construct one	1, 2, 3, 4	Small/indiv.	Construction	1/2 day	All	L/R	Sci 5-13
10. Hot air balloons	Research the history of them	1, 3	Small/indiv.	Reading	1 hr.	Reading/Soc. St.	L	Original
11. Kites	Kite Making	1, 4	Indiv./small	Construction	1/2 day	Art/Sci	L/R	Sci 5-13
12. Kites	Chinese Style	3, 4	Indiv./small	Const/reading	1/2 day	Art/Sci/Soc. St.	L/R	Sci 5-13
13. Fantasies	Body movement about flight	4	Large	Movement	1 hr.	Drama	R	Original
14. Model Rockets	Building	1, 2	Indiv./small	Construction	2 hr.	Math/Sci.	L/R	Estes Co.
15. Model Rockets	Launching (measuring)	2	Indiv./small	Field trip experiment	2 hr.	Math/Sci.	L/R	Estes Co.
16. Rockets	History of them	3	Indiv./small	Reading	1 hr.	Reading/Soc. St.	L	Original
17. Space Travel	"Man in Space"	1, 3	Large	Movie	1 hr.	Sci/Soc. St.	L	NASA films
18. Fantasy	People from other planets	1, 4	Indiv./small	Fantasy trips	2 hrs.	Drama	R	Original

Generalizing Activities

Sub-theme	Activity	Goal #	Size Group	Learning Model	Time	Disciplines	Brain Hemisphere	Source
1. Space Travel	Visit from NASA	1	Large	Lecture, movie	1/2 day	Sci/Soc. St.	L	NASA

2. Presentations by various groups on sub-themes investigated.
3. Open house for parents.

Step 13. Develop detailed lesson plans for each activity.

While there are several forms of lesson planning, most should at least indicate the students' objectives for doing the activity (these should relate directly to the broad goals of the unit), the approximate length of time for the activity, the type of learning mode required of the activity (interview, demonstration, discussion, experiment, slide or movie, lecture, writing, reading, field trip, simulation, game, programmed instruction, construction, etc.), the size group which can do the activity at one time, and resources and materials needed to conduct the activity. If the unit is meant to be interdisciplinary and relate to both hemispheres of the brain, there should be some mention, as well, as to which disciplines are represented by the activity and some indication of whether the activity is predominantly left, right, or mixed dominant. Finally, procedures for conducting the activity should be outlined. If work sheets, task cards, or guide sheets are required, these should also be produced.

Example: Sample Lesson Plan

Balloon Messages

Introductory Lesson

Objectives

A. Children will be able to demonstrate group cooperation skills in designing and constructing a balloon.

B. Children will be able to construct a balloon from the materials provided that will hold helium.

C. Children will be able to write a paragraph each telling about themselves and their project which is to be sent up in their balloon.

Time—One hour

Learning Modes—Construction and writing

Size group—Teams of 3 to 5 children

Materials

A plastic cleaner's bag for each group (preferably brightly colored ones)
Helium
Tape and glue
Scissors
Writing Paper

Disciplines—Science, Math, Language Arts

Brain Hemispheres—Both

Procedures—

A. Discuss ways of using flying things to convey messages to other people. Tell the children they will be making a balloon to fill with helium to send up on the school site. Ask what kind of information and message they would like to send.

B. Provide each group of 3 to 5 children with materials to construct their balloon. Directions can either be very specific or open ended to allow them to discover their own best methods of doing this. If open-ended you should have extra cleaner's bags for those groups who are unsuccessful on their first attempts.

C. Once balloons are constructed have each group produce a message to be placed inside their balloon. The messages should at least contain the date and a return address so that if the balloon is found by someone a message about its finding can be returned.

D. You should then fill each balloon with helium. The balloons should be checked again for leaks. Once ready the balloons should be taken outside for launching.

E. A final discussion can be held as to the launch. Which directions did the balloons appear to be heading? How high did they go? (Mathematics of estimating and calculating heights can be brought in.)

F. Finally, predictions can be made as to how far away from school the balloons will get? How many will be found? How many messages will be returned?

G. Follow-up. Wait and see what happens. Possibilities are in mapping and measuring distances traveled, figuring flight speed, analyzing returned messages and in writing additional messages back to those who were kind enough to respond to the found balloons.

Step 14. Determine procedures for monitoring students involvement and progress.

One underlying assumption about a unit that has several alternative activities to choose from is that not all children will do the same activities. While this takes extra planning, it does allow children to make decisions about what activities to investigate that meet their learning needs and preferences. The system described below should prove helpful, however, in monitoring the progress of each student as they set out investigating different things related to the unit. The system is called a Dart Board Technique[4] and its use will help insure children's involvement in several disciplines and learning modes and for you to keep track of the progress children are making, and to be able to tell at any one time on which activities or sub-themes any child is engaged.

The chart consists of rings with each ring representing a different week of the unit. Week One is the center ring. The circles from Week Two to Week Five are divided like a pie and each segment represents a different discipline. Even though most activities and sub-themes are interdisciplinary they usually have a focus in one of the disciplines. Dividing the chart into discipline segments allows you to see which disciplines are emphasized by the students activities, to communicate to fellow teachers, parents, and administrators which disciplines were incorporated, and to more effectively plan future units to emphasize those disciplines that received little attention in this unit.

Week One consists of the *Introductory* activities which all children will complete. Notice the pie lines do not extend into the first week because there is plenty of overlap in the disciplines this week. The main goals of Week One are to acquaint children with the entire scope of the unit and to permit them opportunities to begin to make decisions about which sub-themes and *Alternative* activities they would like to pursue in Week Two.

During Week Two work on *Alternative* activities begins and children's choices of alternatives are placed in the appropriate segment of the Dart Board. See the example which follows.

In Weeks Three through Four there are more and more alternatives for children and the chart therefore has more space. Children can choose to continue projects started in earlier weeks or move on to new sub-themes within other discipline areas. Here the chart is helpful in giving you information to help guide the child in appropriate directions.

The fifth and final week of the unit is not on the chart because *Generalizing* activities which all children will do are conducted. The concluding activities are designed to provide an opportunity for children to share and express what they have done and found out with their alternative activities and for the children to generalize their learnings to different but related situations.

Example:

"Up, Up, and Away"

Dart Board Technique of
Unit Monitoring

Step 15. *Implement the Unit*

This is the fun part. Go for it! While planning is complete at this point there are some additional things to consider before, during, and after implementation of the unit. The next two chapters provide information on resources, strategies, and methodologies for planning, managing, instructing, and monitoring once the unit has begun.

Conclusion

It has been assumed in this chapter that you as the teacher are the most knowledgeable and capable person for determining what should be taught and how it should be taught to your children in your classroom. What person knows the children more than you? What person knows the home life and views of the parents more than you? What person knows the goals, curriculum materials, and other resources of the school system and school more than you?

The thematic unit approach described in this chapter allows you to draw upon your knowledge and skills to create the most appropriate learning experiences for your children. Rather than starting from scratch in curriculum planning, as this chapter might suggest, you already have many good ideas about appropriate themes that are drawn from existing reading, math, science, language arts, and social studies materials and from existing state, district, and school guidelines. The difference with this approach is that *you* are determining the curriculum rather than accepting what textbook publishers say are "good" curriculums for children and a school they know nothing about.

The use of thematic units also permits you to more effectively integrate learning experiences to correspond to the integrated realities of the child's world.

Notes

1. The Center for Unified Science Education, "Stages in Designing a Modular Unit," Mimeographed Document, The Ohio State University, June, 1975.
2. Alex Osborn from *Applied Imagination* as quoted in *The Universal Traveler,* Don Koberg and Jim Bognall, (Los Altos, California: William Kanfmann, Inc.) 1976, page 68.
3. The Center for Unified Science Education, *Op. cit.,* page 8.
4. From a talk given by Ed Catherall at Arizona State University, July, 1978. Ed Catherall is a science educator from University of Sussex, Sussex, England and one of the authors of *Teaching 5 to 13 Projects* by MacDonald Educational.

Chapter 4

Resources for Developing Outdoor Education Thematic Units

Introduction

There are many sources containing ideas that teachers can utilize to generate activities for the use of the outdoors with children. Unfortunately many of these sources present outdoor education from the point of view of a single discipline, such as science, mathematics, or recreation. As has been suggested in previous chapters this is not representative of the interdisciplinary nature of outdoor education. Nor do many of the available resources attempt to provide ideas and suggestions that provide a balance of right and left brain activities. Thus, teachers will have to either modify many of the existing outdoor education curriculum materials or develop their own.

The programs and materials described in this chapter, however, are representative of the more appropriate and widely available existing outdoor education resources. Familiarity with these programs will provide a solid basis for selecting activities to use with many of the thematic units that relate in some way to the outdoors.

Some Exemplary Outdoor Education Resources

1. *Arizona Teachers Resource Guide for Environmental Education* is a good example of a resource developed by a state department of education for the teachers within a given state. The broad goal of the guide is to help teachers teach the concept that man is an inseparable, integral part of a system that consists of man, culture, and the natural environment and that man has the ability to alter the interrelationships of this system.

The guide provides ideas and activities along with substantial background information for teachers that can be used to supplement and enrich the entire curriculum. The guide is divided into units related to the following resources: air, man in the environment, plants, rocks and minerals, soils, water, and wildlife. Further subdivisions are by grade level and curricular area. Activities are provided for grades one through twelve.

By providing activity suggestions from the various disciplines, a teacher can easily teach environmental concepts by utilizing activities that encourage functions of both sides of the brain; i.e., poetry writing suggestions (right brain), and science experiences (left brain) can be found scattered throughout the guide.

The Arizona guide is available from the Arizona State Department of Education, 1535 West Jefferson, Phoenix, Arizona, 85007.

2. *Broad Spectrum* is an example of a resource developed by a regional environmental education center. The goal of the materials is to help children understand basic ecological concepts, explore environmental problems, and develop positive attitudes toward the environment.

The program consists of two packets of activity cards (primary and intermediate grades) and teacher's guides which provide interdisciplinary experiences in outdoor-environmental education.

Each card is designed to be used by either a child or adult and has several suggested activities related to a central topic or theme. The cards need not be used in any sequence and selection of appropriate cards and activities is left up to the adult.

The whole child can be involved in this program because the cards provide activity based experiences in helping children learn cooperation skills and concepts from social studies, science, art, math, and language arts. Quite often art or drama activities (right brain) are used to introduce or follow-up a left brain type of experience.

Broad Spectrum materials are available from the Center for Environmental Learning, 615 Seminole Drive, Rockledge, Florida, 32955.

3. *The Centering Book* and *The Second Centering Book* are two books specifically designed to provide sources of ideas to help parents and teachers develop children's creative and intuitive capabilities.

The activities contained in these two books can be used to integrate principles of right brain learning into the standard curriculum of the school. Suggestions for using meditation, dreams, fantasy, and other techniques to help children become relaxed, alert, and whole are incorporated. Many of the activities can take place in the informal relaxed environment of the outdoors.

The two centering books can be purchased from most book stores. The authors are Gay Hendricks and Thomas B. Roberts. Publisher is Spectrum Books from Prentice-Hall, Inc., Englewood Cliffs, New Jersey, 07632.

4. *Elementary Science Study* is designed to be an entire elementary science program or a series of disjoint units and activities that can be used to supplement an existing science program for grades kindergarten through eight. While the program covers all areas of science many of the separate units make use of the outdoor environment as the primary teaching resource. Such units include topics on Animal Activity, Earthworms, Tadpoles, Tracks, Butterflies, Crayfish, Water Flow, Pond Water, Budding Twigs, Daytime Astronomy, the Moon, Growing Seeds, Light and Shadows, Mapping, and Rocks and Charts.

Each unit has a guide for the teacher which identifies possible activities, materials needed, and samples of children's ideas and work who have already done the activities. Many of the units also have kits of materials which contain equipment not readily available to a teacher.

While these units differ widely they share a common approach to learning which is designed to enhance left and right brain functioning. Rather than start with a discussion of basic concepts involving the topic, children are first involved with materials (physical or living) so they can acquire in a holistic manner a great deal of useful information and problem solving skills through their own active participation.

Elementary Science Study units are available from the Education Development Center, 55 Chapel Street, Newton, Massachusetts, 02160 or from the publisher, McGraw-Hill Book Company, Webster Division, New York, New York.

5. *Environmental Studies or Essentia* materials are perhaps the most right brain materials available for children. The goal of the program is to provide experiences for children to deal with man's relationship to his natural and man-made surroundings, including relationships to the social, scientific, mathematical, artistic, psychological, and literacy aspects of that environment and to the child.

The program contains two sets of activity cards that can be used by the adult or child. Each card has an assignment or challenge that is purposefully ambigiously stated. This means the child will have to invent their own understanding of the problem and then invent their own solution. An example of two of the challenges are: "Go outside and find a million of something and be able to prove it" and "Find something you really dislike in the classroom or school . . . and see what you can do to change it."

The right brain is heavily involved at the problem identification and problem solving stages in this program. Holistic understandings and intuition are required to understand what is expected in these types of challenges. Furthermore, many of the activities require children to again use the right brain to express (poetry, art, photography, song, etc.) the results of the activity they have completed.

Environmental Studies or Essentia materials are available from the publisher, Addison-Wesley Publishing Co., Innovative Division, Sand Hill Road, Menlo Park, California, 94025.

6. *The New Games Book* is a resource of ideas, activities, and games for parents and teachers to use in providing opportunities for people of all ages to participate in the process of playing hard, having fun, with everybody winning and nobody getting hurt. Many of the games can be played competitively, with lots of opportunity for skill, cooperation, and strategy. Others have no object besides getting people together and enjoying each other. There are games that can be played in groups of two to one hundred.

The significance of this resource for the development of the whole child is that the child can become physically involved in play and imagination with the environment and other people. As George Leonard, one of the creators of New Games said, "Everybody has rediscovered their bodies and imaginations. People experience the joy of playing together."[1]

Because many of the games are for outdoor play, there are also many opportunities to develop concern for and appreciation of the outdoor environment. One of the major goals of the book is to make people aware of public lands and to promote interest in maintaining them and using them in an ecologically sound manner.

The New Games Book can be purchased in most book stores or from the New Games Foundation, P.O. Box 7901, San Francisco, California, 94120, or from the publisher, A Headlands Press Book, San Francisco, California. The book was printed in 1976 and edited by Andrew Fluefelman.

7. *Outdoor Biology Instructional Strategies* is a program that offers ten to fifteen year old children investigations emphasizing the use of various environments such as city lots, local parks, streams, forests, ponds, the desert, and sea shore. Most of the activities have been designed for use by non-science oriented people including community-sponsored youth organizations and schools that use the outdoors as a learning laboratory. The primary goal of *OBIS* is to help children and leaders better understand and appreciate ecological relationships in their local environment.

There are four separate packets of activity cards, and each activity may be used independently or sequenced to create a larger program to suit individual needs. Each activity card identifies background information for the adult, a list of materials required, information on how to prepare for the activity, a detailed lesson plan, and possible follow-up activities.

The *OBIS* program makes a significant contribution to the development of the whole child because most of the activities start with some kind of right brain activity (such as a craft or art project, game, or simulation). These high interest and high participatory inquiry activities lead to understandings about the environment and help develop children's decision making skills.

OBIS is available from the Lawrence Hall of Science, University of California, Berkeley, California, 94720.

8. *Science Curriculum Improvement Study* is another program designed to be an entire elementary science curriculum for grades kindergarten to six. The program has two large units at each grade level designed to last the whole school year. One unit is in physical-earth science and the other is in life science. Both units make extensive use of the outdoors as a learning laboratory. In particular, the life science units for the various grade levels focus on the concepts of organisms, life cycles, populations, environments, communities, and ecosystems.

Within each unit there are teacher's guides, student guides, and kits of materials which contain several activities for children to do to explore materials and concepts, learn concepts and skills, and discover new applications of these skills and concepts. While the program is meant to be used somewhat in sequence, many teachers have been able to extract particular subunits or activities to supplement other programs, units, or themes in outdoor education.

SCIS contributes to the development of the whole child because of its emphasis on learning by doing and thinking about what has been done. Despite the structure in the program there is adequate flexibility for children to use drawing, poetry, music, and drama to help both halves of the brain better understand and express the concepts that are taught.

SCIS materials are now available in their second edition from at least two publishers: Rand McNally and Company, Box 7600, Chicago, Illinois, 60680 for the *SCIIS* version and from the American Science and Engineering, 20 Overland Street, Boston, Massachusetts, 02215, for the *SCIS II* version.

9. *Science 5–13* is designed to be used with children ranging in age from five to thirteen. While the program could be used as a total science program there is no specified sequence of activities to follow. Such a sequence would have to be determined by the teacher. The main use of the materials is to provide "starter" ideas for activities which revolve around themes that are inherently interesting for children. Rather than sticking just with science activities, the suggestions lend themselves well to the integration of all disciplines. The over-all goal of the program is to help children develop inquiry and critical thinking skills.

The program only contains teacher's guides, each of which is on a different theme. Within each guide several suggestions are given about activities that children can do to investigate the various themes and subthemes. The guides and themes which rely heavily on the use of the outdoors are as follows: Like and Unlike, Colored Things, Structures and Forces, Change, Time, Holes, Gaps and Cavities, Minibeasts, Ourselves, and Trees. In addition to these units there is also a special set of units that deal exclusively with outdoor education. In this latter set there are six guide books for leading children's investigations in the outdoors.

Science 5–13 was designed for use in schools in Great Britain but is now available in the United States from Raintree Childrens Books, 205 W. Highland Avenue, Milwaukee, Wisconsin, 53203.

10. *Unified Science and Mathematics for Elementary Schools* has as its primary goal the development of children's problem solving skills. The integration of science and mathematics is the vehicle for solving real and practical problems from the local school/community environment. While the program can be used as a total mathematics and science curriculum it also lends itself well as a supplement to existing programs and to outdoor education efforts.

The program has separate units which are all based on a challenge which presents the problem that is both real and practical to children. The units that have an emphasis on the outdoors as a laboratory are called Traffic Flow, Pedestrian Crossings, Burglar Alarm Design, Play Area Design and Use and Weather Predictions, Advertising, Bicycle Transportation, and Nature Trails.

The *USMES* program presents problem solving from an interdisciplinary approach, thus meeting the definition of outdoor education and also provides a variety of opportunities for children to learn left and right brain problem solving strategies.

USMES materials are available from the Educational Development Center, 55 Chapel Street, Newton, Massachusetts, 02160.

Additional Resources

The following resources are included because of their value in providing ideas and suggestions for conducting activities in the outdoors with children on a variety of themes. Some of the books and publications provide activity suggestions on limited themes such as "Winter Activities" and others attempt to deal with several themes. Annotations are provided to indicate the types of themes discussed.

Resources which deal with general philosophical or methological aspects of outdoor education are not included. Neither are resources which could be called "field guides" on various aspects of outdoor content included.

Finally, no attempt has been made to review all possible activity-based resources. Rather, the intent has been to provide a representative sample of resources which originate from a variety of governmental, private, and public sources.

Ashbaugh, Byron L. and Kordish, Raymond J., *Trail Planning and Lay-out,* National Audubon Society, 1971, 76 pgs. A guide to planning, building, and maintaining nature trails. Includes information on types of trails, signs, interpretation, activities, etc.

Ashbaugh, Byron L., *Planning A Nature Center,* National Audubon Society, 1973, 98 pgs. Covers all aspects of planning for a nature center including rationale, facilities, funding, staffing, operation, and possible curriculum and activities.

Association of Classroom Teachers, *Man and His Environment,* NEA and AHPE and R, 1972, 56 pgs. Approaches environmental education through the use of five concept themes: Variety and Similarity, Patterns, Interaction and Interdependence, Continuity and Change, and Adaptation and Evolution. Suggestions are provided for incorporating these concept themes into all subject areas of the curriculum.

Bachert, Russel E. Jr., and Snooks, Emerson L., *Outdoor Education Equipment,* The Interstate Printers and Publishers, Inc., 1974, 205 pgs. A collection of directions and patterns for constructing instructional aids to be used in the outdoors. Aids for the following themes are discussed: animal life, math, water, weather, soil, and miscellaneous.

Bale, Robert O., *What On Earth,* American Camping Association, 1969, A bit of Earth's history introduces skills and projects involving nature lore.

Bengtsson, Arvid, *Environmental Planning for Children's Play,* Praeger Publishers, 1970, 224 pgs. A comprehensive survey of playgrounds in the U.S., Canada, Europe, and Japan. Among topics treated are climate, housing, redevelopment of old areas, portable playgrounds, gardens, zoos, various types of play (sand, water, adventure), festival streets, malls, and play areas for adults as well as children. It provides suggestions for the development and use of such areas by parents, educators, and all those active in community affairs.

Brehm, Shirley A., *A Teacher's Handbook for Study Outside the Classroom,* Charles E. Merrill Publishing Co., 1969, 100 pgs. Ideas about the organization of field trips: planning, transportation, resources, places to visit, classroom follow-up, suggested activities, and evaluation.

Brennan, Mathew J., *People and Their Environment,* J.C. Ferguson Publishing Co., 1969. Teacher's Curriculum Guides to Conservation Education. Series of eight books: Grades 1-2-3, Grades 4-5-6, Science 7-8-9, Social Studies 7-8-9, Social Studies 10-11-12, Home Economics 9-12, Biology, and Outdoor Laboratory 1-12.

Brown, Robert E. and Mouser, G.W.,*Techniques for Teaching Conservation Education,* Burgess Publishing Co., 1964, 112 pgs. A handbook covering conservation principles, methodology for field trips, field experiences, and a bibliography.

Brown, Vinson, *The Amateur Naturalist's Handbook,* Little Brown and Co., 1948. A handbook for beginning, intermediate, and advanced naturalists, including various activities and suggestions for observations, collecting, and keys to plants, animals, and rocks.

Brown, Vinson, *Knowing the Outdoors in the Dark,* MacMillan Co., 1973. A very helpful manual for identifying sights, smells in the dark and developing one's sixth sense (could this be a right brain sense).

Comstock, Anna B., *Handbook of Nature Study 24th Edition,* Comstock Publishing Associates 1939. A classic guide to field studies and natural environments. Seven hundred investigation ideas and a list of resources also provided.

Cutler, Katherine N., *From Petals to Pine Cones: A Nature Art and Craft Book,* Lothrop Co., 1969. Selecting natural materials, pressing and drying, individual and school projects, shows, and reference. A good how-to book. For use by student and teachers planning ideas.

Disley, John, *Orienteering,* Stackpole Books, 1973. Introduction to the sport of orienteering with map and compass techniques.

Educational Facilities Laboratories, *Environmental Education/Family Resources,* 1973, 64 pgs. A resource for school site development plans, community facilities and programs, regional centers, camps, and programs-in-the making to spur rural and urban involvement in processes of man's life cycle.

Environmental Education Center, *Valuing the Environment,* 1658 Sterling Road, Charlotte, N.C., 28209. This is an interdisciplinary approach to the environment that uses environmental packets that emphasize value clarification. In this project teachers use hands-on materials and field work to assist children (ages 6 through 11) in understanding and valuing their environment.

Garrison, Cecil, *Outdoor Education: Principles and Practice,* C.C. Thomas, 1966. A manual for community, scout, camp, family, and school participation in outdoor education.

Gross, Phyllis P. and Railton, Esther P., *Teaching Science in an Outdoor Environment.* Parents, teachers, and camp leaders, and student handbook. University of California Press, 1972, 188 pgs. Short outdoor education units, providing questions, equipment lists, and concepts to develop for each unit.

Humann, Julianna M., *Environmental Education: A Teacher's Guide with Inquiry and Value Seeking Strategies,* Jackson Publishing Co., 1973. A curricular plan of discussions and activities with textbooks, projects, experiments, drawings, etc., to foster understanding physical and social interaction. Appendix on films, references, eco-concern organizations, suggestions and glossary.

Hamilton, Charles E., *ECO,* Educational Service, Inc., 1974, 185 pgs. A handbook written for elementary teachers to stimulate students to an awareness of the environment. Material is available examining various parts of the environment including: soil, air, water, etc. Discussion topics related to the interrelatedness between our environment and everyday life are also presented.

Hindman, Darwin A., *Games and Stunts,* Prentice Hall, Inc., 1956, 415 pgs. A complete collection of games both athletic and "parlor." The games are presented in a detailed, logical classification system based on their fundamental principles and ideas. Several suggestions are provided for activities and games children can do on busses and in cars while on route to outdoor sites.

Kjellstrom, Bjorn, *Be Expert with Map and Compass,* Scriber's Sons, 1967. Map and compass theories for yourself and for teaching with specific practices-self testing and group projects. Includes practicing compass, protractor, and map.

Knapp, Clifford *Outdoor Activities for Environmental Studies,* The Instructor Publications, 1971, pgs 48. A handbook of environmental investigations for various age groups. Contents include measurements, hypsometers, clinometers, moving water, soil compaction, wind speed, sundials, etc.

Laurel Ecology Center, *Model Educational Program in Ecology,* 1044 No. Hayworth Ave., Los Angeles, California, 90046. The development and implementation of a comprehensive and sequential ecology program from kindergarten through adult education has been the goal of this project. The suggested learning strategies for children emphasize a large number of individualized experiences that are keyed to various ecological concepts.

Levitt, Marshall, *Star Maps for Beginners,* Simon and Schuster, 1964, 47 pgs. The easiest system of star charts yet devised for locating the major constellations and planets in the northern hemisphere at any time of year.

MacBean, John C., Stecher, Adam, Wentworth, Daniel F., Couchman, Kenneth J., *Examining Your Environment Series,* Holt, Rinehart and Winston of Canada, Limited, 1972. A series of twelve books including activities on a main theme with follow-up sections after each chapter that guide children toward a deeper understanding of the concepts and skills involved. Book titles are as follows: Astronomy, Birds, Ecology, Mapping Small Places, Miniclimates, Pollution, Running Water, Small Creatures, Snow and Ice, The Dandelion, Trees, and Your Senses.

Marsh, Norman F., *Outdoor Education on Your School Grounds,* 1967. A guide to school site development, utilization of the outdoor laboratory, teaching strategies and important ideas for effective learning strategies.

Milliken, Margaret, *Field Study Manual for Outdoor Learning,* Burgess Publishing Co., 1968. A manual of suggested projects, work sheets, resources for outdoor learning experiences.

Musselman, Virginia W., *Learning About Nature Through Crafts,* Stackpole Books, 1969, 128 pgs. Over 150 ideas for craft projects using natural media.

Musselman, Virginia W., *Learning About Nature Through Games,* Stackpole Books, 1967, 120 pgs. A book of ideas for awareness games and projects, sensory experiences, science projects, and a list of resources.

Mustard, Major C.A., *By Map and Compass-An Introduction to Orienteering,* MacMillan Co. of Canada Ltd., 1950. Basics of map-making and reading and using the compass by useful exercises. Study maps included.

National Audubon Society, *A Place to Live,* 950 Third Avenue, New York, NY 10022. This includes a student's edition and teacher's manual which provides a "mini-course" in ecology for urban children. Included are instructional activities which invite children to investigate their environment and background and factual information for the children and adults using the guide.

National Park Foundation and National Park Service, *Outdoor Book: Adventure in Environment,* Silver Burdett Co. Ten lessons for sixth grade children involving such varied themes as kite flying, and adaptation or evolution but interconnected with interdisciplinary concepts and principles; one of three books (outdoor, classroom, and teacher's guide) available for grades 3 through 6.

National Wildlife Federation, *Environmental Discovery Units,* 1412 Sixteenth Street, N.W., Washington, D.C. 20036. A series of 24 booklets, each approximately 20 pgs. Inquiry oriented, self-contained teacher guides covering a wide range of topics and organized to help teachers lead students from low to higher skills and concepts. Activities which call for easily obtained materials promise to nurture lasting interests in the environment. Representative titles are: Man's Habitat, The City, Fish and Water Temperature, The Rise and Fall of a Yeast Community, and Oaks, Acorns, Climate, and Squirrels.

Nickelsburg, Janet, *Nature Activities for Early Childhood,* Addison-Wesley Publishing Co., 1976, 158 pgs. A book of 44 projects for parents and teachers designed to provide young children with experiences in observing nature. It is planned to assist in developing skill in observation, improvement of speech, and expansion of their aesthetic appreciations. Activity sections are included as well as lists of helpful materials, and key vocabulary words for children. There is a bibliography at the end of each chapter with lists of books which describe things of nature in simple terms.

Olsen, Larry Dean, *Outdoor Survival Skills,* Bringham Young University Press, 1973, 188 pgs. A book dealing with a wide variety of outdoor survival skills including chapters on shelter, fire, water, plants, animals, and special skills.

Paul, Aileen, *Kids Camping,* Doubleday and Co., 1973, 141 pgs. A camping book for kids with chapters on planning your trip, camping gear, backpacking, camping by the sea, camping in Canada and Mexico. It also suggests a menu and grocery list for four people for seven days. A good guide for parents wishing to work with their children.

Petzoldt, Paul, *The Wilderness Handbook,* W.W. Norton and Co., 1974, 286 pgs. A book on the conservation of the individual, his equipment and the environment. Section on gear is thoroughly discussed. Trail techniques, the necessity for good expedition behavior, camping conservation, basic climbing, and specialized information on summer snow techniques and winter mountaineering are stressed. This is perhaps the best resource for adults and leaders wishing to take groups into the outdoors for more than one day.

Project Learning Tree, American Forest Institute, Inc. A program designed to be used with children in a certain region of the United States. The focus of the two teacher's manuals (K-6 and 7-12) is to provide activities that help children in Western United States understand their interdependence with the total forest community. The activities are drawn from all school disciplines including the arts, science, mathematics, and social studies.

Ris, Thomas F., Editor, *Energy and Man's Environment,* Education/Research Systems Inc., 1974, 112 pgs. A curriculum guide of activities for elementary through high school grades. Several first-hand activities on the theme of energy are suggested. The following sub-themes are included in the activity section: uses of energy, sources of energy, conversion of energy, environmental impact of energy sources and uses, limits of the earth, and future energy sources.

Sale, Lee and Lee, E., *Environmental Education in the Elementary School,* Holt, Rinehart and Winston, 1972. Includes sections on philosophy of environmental education, areas and methods of instruction, a section on survival all interspersed with activity suggestions, and ideas for projects and resources to use.

Shomon, Joseph J., *Manual of Outdoor Conservation Education,* National Audubon Society, 1964, 96 pgs. Includes information on program planning, rationale and philosophy, teaching techniques, facilities and materials, and administration.

Soil Conservation Service, *Conservation and the Water Cycle,* SCS, Information Division, Washington, D.C., 20250, Color diagram and brief description of the water cycle and its relationship to soil, plants, animals, and man's management of water resources.

Soil Conservation Service, *Conservation in Elementary Schools, An Outline for Teaching,* SCS, Information Division, Washington, D.C. 20250, 14 pgs. Provides general objectives for environmental education, list of things to do, and list of things to talk about for grades 1–8. Includes graded reading list.

Soil Conservation Service, *The Measure of our Land,* SCS, Information Division, Washington, D,C,, 20250, 22 pgs. Nontechnical explanation of how soil scientists study land forms and the characteristics of soil layers in order to classify land as a guide for land use planning and management.

Soil Conservation Service, *Outdoor Classrooms on School Sites,* SCS, Information Division, Washington, D.C., 20250, 24 pgs. How to develop opportunities to observe, measure, classify, and interpret the interaction and relationships among living things and their natural environments. Includes many pictures of students involved in environmental study activities.

Soil Conservation Service, *Soil and Water Conservation, A Classroom and Field Guide for Teaching,* SCS, Information Division, Washington, D.C. 20250, 30 pgs. Describes 22 practical activities to help young people understand the interaction of many phenomena in their environment and the need for wise conservation practices to prevent damage to natural resources.

Smith, Julian W., *Outdoor Education,* American Association for Health, Physical Education, and Recreation, 1956 and 1970, 32 pgs. A phamphlet which includes a section on outdoor education philosophy, activities in the outdoors which integrate math, language arts, social studies, biological sciences, earth science, health, physical education, arts, crafts, and music. It also suggests a sample elementary outdoor school program.

Stapp, William B., and Cox, Dorothy A., *Environmental Education Activities Manual,* from Dorothy Cox, 30808 LaMar, Farmington Hills, Michigan, 48024, 1975, 1016 pgs. The manual of activities was designed by students and teachers in environmental education workshops. Volume I includes a philosophy of environmental education, a model and guide for implementation, a resource materials list, and an index to activities. Volumes II–VI include grade level activities developing the concepts of ecosystem, population, economics and technology, environmental decisions, and environmental ethics.

Swan, Malcolm D., *Tips and Tricks in Outdoor Education,* The Inter-State Printers and Publishers, Inc., 1970, 184 pgs. Suggestions for projects in all aspects of outdoor education on mapping, arts, biology, geology, water, recreation, awareness, and a rationale for outdoor education.

Troost, Cornelius J, and Altman, Harold, *Environmental Education: A Sourcebook,* Wiley, 1972. A compilation of readings, activities, field trips, projects, etc., followed by a glossary and bibliography.

U.S. Forest Service, *Environmental Education for Teachers and Resource People,* U.S. Department of Agriculture. This comprehensive guide suggests investigations designed for an in-depth look at different components of the environment including: the forest, soil, water quality, measuring the environment, and range management. Complete lesson plans provide a structure to learning progressing from one activity and concept to a higher, more complex idea. Each lesson plan includes processes involved, self-directed task cards, discussion questions, analysis charts and tables, summarizing questions, and behavioral outcomes. The remainder of the guide is a training manual for the implementation of environmental education programs.

Van der Smissen, Betty, and Goerng, Oswald H., *A Leader's Guide to Nature Oriented Activities,* Iowa State University Press, 1965, 218 pgs. Part 1 covers the development and organization of an outdoor program and Part 2 suggests various activities, including nature crafts, games, and outdoor living skills.

Van Matre, Steve, *Acclimatization,* American Camping Association, 1972, 138 pgs. A unique approach to environmental studies which emphasizes right brain approaches for children of all ages. Activities involve sensory approaches to the learning of ecological concepts. Lesson plans and techniques are included.

Van Matre, Steve, *Acclimatizing,* American Camping Association, 1974, 225 pgs. Continues the essence of methods of acclimatization; ideas for programs with new sensory awareness activities.

Vivian, Eugene V., *Sourcebook for Environmental Education,* C.V. Mosby Co., 1973, 206 pgs. A series of units with lesson plans ranging from primary to secondary grade levels requiring from 3 to 8 weeks of class time is presented. Activities and data-collection work sheets are provided in detail sufficient to allow for use by teachers or students. Lesson plans relate to the following environmental factors; air, water, and solid waste pollution. Biological and physical sciences are integrated with aspects of mathematics, geography, government, and politics.

Weaver, Elbert C., Editor, *Scientific Experiments in Environmental Pollution,* Manufacturing Chemists Association, Holt Rinehart and Winston, Inc., 42 pgs. Estimating total acids in air, counting radioactive particles in air, building an electric precipitator, detection of traces of flouride ions in water or other substances, and 14 other activities designed to increase awareness of environmental pollution problems and some of the difficulties involved in seeking solution are presented in this book. Student manuals and teacher's manual are appropriate for grades 8–12.

Weaver, Richard L, *Manual for Outdoor Laboratories,* Interstate Publishers and Printers, 1959, 81 pgs. A collection of readings on various activities, projects, and stragegies for student and teacher involved in the development and use of the school grounds as outdoor laboratories for teaching science and conservation.

Wigginton, Eliot, *The Foxfire Book* (series), Doubleday, 1972. Each of the four books in the series is a collection of "how-to's," stories, remedies, and other myths and realities of Appalachian life. Excellent resource for pioneer or environmental living programs and themes.

Youngpeter, John M., *Winter Science Activities,* Holiday House, 1966, 128 pgs. A book which is appropriate to the United States and Canada. It presents some seventy winter time experiments and projects concerning protozoa, snails, insects, seeds, small plants, deciduous and evergreen trees, temperatures and weather, soils, water, ice, frost, and snow, the stars and the sun.

Conclusion

As mentioned previously, the programs and sources described here are but a few of those available to teachers. Even though many could be classified as predominately science or environmental education in nature, they are flexibly enough designed to allow a teacher to integrate the ideas with other areas of the curriculum and to promote left and right brain thinking and doing if a thematic approach to planning for such integration is used.

Notes

1. Leonard, George, *The New Games Book,* A Headlands Press Book, San Francisco, California, 1976, page 13.

Chapter 5

Ways and Means

Introduction

While outdoor education activities require the same application of good principles of indoor teaching, there are some planning, management, and teaching techniques that are different for the outdoors. Despite the differences, however, it is important to realize that the policies and procedures of the school system protect, guide, and support all educational activities, whether they occur in or away from the school building or school site. Instructional policies pertaining to health, safety, legal provisions, liability and other aspects of the educational structure follow the learners and teachers to the environments which are conducive to the achievement of educational objectives prescribed by the local, state, and federal agencies responsible for education.

This chapter identifies effective strategies for planning outdoor education experiences, suggestions for managing children in the outdoors and discusses various teaching behaviors, methodologies, and techniques of instruction and evaluation.

Policies of health, instruction and liability follow the teacher and children anywhere in the outdoors, even to the Grand Canyon.

It is possible many reading this book feel uncomfortable thinking about taking children in the outdoors. This is a natural feeling for many teachers and parents but is one that is easy to overcome. The first step in overcoming this fear is to attempt to identify the source of the fear. Perhaps you are just uncomfortable in the outdoors, whether leading children or not. This feeling may be due to the separation of our life styles from nature. Unlike our ancestors many of us have grown up with little contact, knowledge, and appreciation of the outdoor environment.

There may be others of you who feel comfortable in the outdoors—perhaps because of a rural upbringing or the fondness of camping and outdoor recreation—but you may not feel knowledgeable enough to lead children in the outdoors because you don't know the names of plants, animals, rocks, and other natural phenomenon that children might ask about. This feeling is easier to overcome. Remember, outdoor education is not science in the outdoors; it is interdisciplinary, involving the processes and concepts of all disciplines as well as providing opportunities to develop left and right brain intellectual skills, social skills, and positive environmental attitudes. Knowing the names of things is not that critical to achieving many of the intellectual, social, and attitudinal goals of education. If a child absolutely has to know the name of something or wants more information than you have there are always resource books or people that have this information.

Planning Outdoor Experiences

Most outdoor education experiences do take extra preparation and time for the teacher and children. Thus, you first must be committed to the fact that the development of students' knowledge, skill, and attitude needed to understand, preserve and intellectually function in and with the environment is worth a little extra effort and time on your part. As you conduct more and more outdoor experiences you'll find the planning time becomes less and the preparation becomes automatic. This section provides an outline of many helpful suggestions for helping to make your outdoor experiences run smoothly.

1. *Have a reason for going outdoors.* Perhaps the most important consideration in planning is to have a recognized need or purpose for going into the outdoors. Furthermore, this reason should relate to the existing goals and objectives of the curriculum. While it is often done, taking children outdoors just for the sake of getting out of the classroom for a period of time, has little justification for the time, energy, and money required to do so. When children are taken outdoors it should be to achieve goals or objectives that cannot be achieved equally well indoors.

Examples of the general kinds of experiences that cannot be provided equally well indoors are as follows:

A. To investigate a specific resource like a garbage can, drainage ditch or construction site which could be parts of units on solid waste, irrigation or water, or on structures and architecture.

B. To develop a better understanding through first hand experience of a concept such as the interaction between plants and animals or the protective coloration of animals.

C. To investigate an environmental problem like air pollution from automobiles or traffic congestion near the school.

D. To provide opportunities to use the higher mental processes involved in problem solving. Examples might be in solving real mathematics problems such as calculating the height of trees, finding a million of something, estimating distances or conducting a controlled experiment.

E. To provide opportunities to experience various outdoor settings which can be the incentive for creative expression in writing, drama, music and art. Observing carefully a tree on the school site can lead, for example, to poetry writing or water coloring.

F. To develop or practice an outdoor leisure time skill such as orienteering (use of map and compass), whether forcasting, archery or bait casting. Incidently, these experiences also provide lots of opportunities to incorporate curriculum areas. For example, archery can involve a great deal of mathematics, science, and social studies.

The skill of bait casting provides opportunities to learn
a leisure time hobby as well as incorporate many
mathematics and science concepts.

G. To develop an appreciation or positive attitude towards some aspect of the outdoor environment. An example might be a night hike to experience the feeling of "nightness" away from the sounds and lights of the city. Many right brain activities can also be tied to these experiences to allow children the opportunity to express their feelings and appreciations about such experiences.

H. To participate in recreational games and sports that allow children to develop social and cooperation skills.

   2. Determine Outdoor Resource Needed. Once the need is identified and rationale given that relates to achieving existing goals and objectives, a decision needs to be made regarding what outdoor resource will best meet this need. Because of the ever present financial limitations those resources that are closest to the school should be considered first. As described in Chapter 1 these resources range from the school site, community resources within one days trip from the school, to trips requiring more than one day away from the school.

3. *Determine How to Utilize the Resource.* Keeping in mind the theme and purpose of the outdoor experience the teacher next needs to determine how to utilize the outdoor resource. Some of the general types of utilizations are as follows:

A. Visiting trip—to explore a site, to seek information and collect data. There may or may not be a resource person or guide available at the site to help provide this information or to guide the exploration. Examples of visiting trips might be trips to the bakery, zoo, or national monument.

B. Collection trip—an extension of a classroom experience where things, drawings, or pictures of things can be brought back to the classroom for study. Examples of this might be a trip to the desert, a pond, or to the forest to collect rocks, leaves, or animals.

C. Field investigation or field study—to investigate a problem, collect data, or construct something. An example of this might be the intensive study of a square meter of lawn, the transit study of a forest area, or a population count of the trees in an area. For this kind of activity the resource can be used for short periods of study over a whole school year.

D. Overnight or school camping experience which could incorporate all of the above types of experiences as well as providing unique opportunities to help develop the social skills of children.

4. *Determine Activities.* The next step is the determination of the specific activities the children will carry out at the outdoor site. This in part will be determined by the thematic planning carried out and the type of trip being conducted. Suggestions and resources described in Chapters 3 and 4 in this book will help provide possible guidelines for planning activities.

5. *Pre-trip Arrangements and Preparing Pupils.* A major step in any planning is the determination of what needs to be done and needed to carry out and follow-up the outdoor experience. The type and extent of the trip will determine which steps from the following outline should be considered:

A. Pre-trip Arrangements

1. Acquire concensus for the trip from teammates and principal.
2. Visit the site to assess the time needed for travel and complete activities, to assess appropriateness for children, to find out whether lavatory accommodation and drinking facilities exist, and to find the nearest point for help in the event of an emergency.
3. Seek permissions to use the facilities, schedule the trip, and schedule resource people connected with the site.
4. Determine how and where transportation will occur.
5. Determine how the trip is financed: children pay all, scholarships, fund raising, school pays.
6. Recruit volunteer help; older students, parents, interested adults, district personnel, other teachers, use of resource people such as school nurse, forest service ranger, game and fish department ranger, etc.

B. Preparing the Pupils

1. Prepare in advance to make sure each child:
    a. Knows what is expected,
    b. Has learned the necessary skills,
    c. Has available the equipment and apparatus required, and
    d. Understands guide and worksheets.
2. Prepare a cover letter for parents. See Appendix A for an example.
3. Prepare permission slips. See Appendix B.
4. Prepare a medical form for students' parents to fill out. See Appendix C.
5. Plan menu and food purchasing list.
6. If an overnight trip, prepare a list of what gear children should bring. See Appendix D.

Organization for an overnight trip also includes proper packing of gear to fit it
onto the bus.

7. Cabin assignments for over night trips.
8. Duties and responsibilities list for teacher, other involved personnel, and students.
9. Insurance forms and payment.
10. Plan a daily schedule. Besides providing a variety of activities—small group, individual, and large group, work time, instructional time, and free time—consideration should also be given for: food preparation, meal clean up, free time after meals, dorm check (clean up inspection), snack time, bed check, "all quiet," and staff planning. See sample schedule, Appendix E.
11. Inform special teachers and cafeteria at school the dates you will be gone.
12. Decide on rules with children. See Sample in Appendix F.

Organizing and Managing the Class Outdoors

Management of children and the learning environment is different in the outdoors because there are not walls and rigid time schedules of the indoor environment. The control of 20 to 30 children for the first time in the outdoors can be a daunting experience, even with the help of a colleague. To organize the class so rigidly that the excitement of going outdoors is lost or the opportunity for individual work and personal involvement is lessened is not desirable. Providing absolute freedom is not better, however. A clamoring bunch around the teacher offers little fruitful work or fun to be accomplished. The following suggestions are offered to provide a happy medium between too rigid and too loose management of children in the outdoors.

It is best to work up gradually to working with children outdoors. Don't haul the children off for an overnight or day long experience if you've never taken a group outdoors before. The following progression has been suggested by teachers:

1. Take the class outside on the school grounds to have a discussion or read a book to the students. Identify with the students' help rules of behavior. Students will begin to get the idea that the outdoors can be used for more than just recess.
2. Have a somewhat structured (work card, task card type) activity for students to do outdoors, again with the focus on rules of behavior and what is required to complete the task in the time required to complete the task. You probably should be outdoors with the children at this time.
3. Do additional activities on the school site for longer and longer periods of time; on each occasion shifting more of the responsibility for behavior and completing the task to the students.
4. Assuming ability of the students and you to function in the above, then you should be ready for ventures away from the school site.

Note: The intent of the above progression is to establish an environment and rapport among teacher and students that communicates, "I know you are capable and trustworthy." Unfortunately, if this same kind of environment and trust cannot or is not established in the classroom then it is doubtful whether it can occur in the outdoors where there aren't the physical and psychological restraints of walls, schedules, books, and tests.

Even after careful planning and a progression of activities as described above you shouldn't expect that your first or even your second "large" outdoor experience will be a complete success. It may take you and the children some time to become acclimated to the different and informal learning environment of the outdoors. There are some further specific suggestions, however, which might help you avoid some of the more subtle pitfalls of working with children in the outdoors.

1. When children are given anything new such as a magnifying glass or book the natural tendency is to explore. Children's exploration not only introduces them to new things but permits them to raise questions and make observations that increase interest in finding out more. The same type of exploration is needed with new outdoor resources. Thus, children should be allowed the opportunity to walk around and observe all the things there are in a new environment before being asked to conduct specific activities. Activities such as a scavenger hunt (see page 74) or directions from the teacher to "see what interesting things you can find" are openings which allow children to meet the need to explore. If children are not given this exploration opportunity they often become side-tracked from the task you've given them because they are finding new things to investigate instead. Such exploration should be within the bounds of safety, however.

2. Once the exploration need has been met the most important management suggestion that can be given is to make sure the children know what is required of them in completing activities and why they are doing these activities. They also must recognize the relevance of the outdoor experience for the indoor curriculum they are studying. Besides understanding from a curriculum point of view they must also understand what is expected from their behavior point of view. If you have already developed rapport and trust with the children they will know they can be responsible and capable of handling themselves in the outdoors without constant supervision from you. There may be some children, however, for whom you will have to prescribe definite limits if they are unable to function with the increased freedom of the outdoors.

3. Don't attempt to do things outdoors that can be better done indoors. In other words don't attempt to hold unnecessary mini-lectures that could be held back indoors afterwards; don't take time instructing and practicing how to use equipment and apparatus—this can be done before hand in the classroom, and don't have students spend unnecessary time looking up names of things when samples can be collected for later reference work in the classroom.

4. Anytime and anywhere you're in the outdoors with a large group of children it is best to have help to reduce the adult-child ratio and to provide a more meaningful experience for each child. It is impossible to be dogmatic about the ideal ratio because this will depend upon the age of the children, the site being used, safety considerations, and the activities you want the pupils to conduct.

When it is advisable to have a lower adult-child ratio there are several people who could be called on to help supervise children including nurses, bus drivers, the principal, older students, volunteer retired people, and other teachers.

With additional help children can be allowed more freedom to work individually or in small groups. When walking on trails or city streets in lines, adults can be evenly distributed among students allowing at least one adult in front, one in the middle and one at the rear of the line to permit ultimate supervision.

Finally, when two or more teachers work together in a team teaching situation, it is possible to achieve greater variety in the size of groups for activities on the school site. This can be accomplished by allowing one teacher to take a few children (example 10–15) for an outdoor activity while the others are divided among the remaining teachers.

5. A more complex organization is required when it is necessary for one adult to work with a whole class in the outdoors.

If you must lead a large group alone doing such things as walking along a nature trail, crossing streets in the city, or visiting a zoo, the best place to be positioned is in the center of the line of children. The group can be kept pretty close together in this manner by selecting the most responsible and respected students to lead and follow the group. If the lead and trail students always remain within shouting distance you can always stop the group and call attention to something. By being in the middle of the group you are always within 20–25 feet of every child. It's much more difficult to maintain control if leading and almost impossible if you're following the group.

There are some additional suggestions that may also pertain whether you are alone with a large group of children or have adult assistance. These are:

6. Identify the physical limits or boundaries within which the children are to operate to conduct their activities. While the activities partially dictate the boundaries they should usually be such that no matter where the children go within the area, they are still within your eye sight. If you feel comfortable allowing children out of your sight then a sound signal such as a bell or whistle can still be used to bring the group back together again.

7. In addition to boundaries it is important to plan and set time limits for completion of activities.

Frequent short expeditions for different purposes provide better learning situations than occasional, long, tiring outings into which a range of experiences are crowded. Suitable periods would be 10–45 minutes on the school site, and between one hour and half a day farther afield.

Even if children don't have watches or can't tell time they still can realize they have about 15 minutes (time of 1/2 of a T.V. show) or 30 minutes (time of most T.V. shows). This allows them the opportunity to gauge the pace of their activities and to return to the starting point at the completion of the activity.

8. Even when it is desirable to keep a group pretty close together while in the outdoors there are ways to permit children some individual freedom to explore or collect data. Again, boundaries and time limits are important, however. For example, while leading a group in a line along a nature trail it is possible to release children from the trail one at a time to explore areas next to the trail, or, if it is a large group, groups of children can be released at intervals. These side trips can be quite short, a matter of a minute or so.

9. There are always possibilities of accidents in the outdoors thus extra planning is needed to prepare children for potential accidents. If, for example, children are away from the group and an accident occurs, the pupils should have been instructed to go to the nearest adult. If one is not in view, two pupils should go, one in each direction looking for an adult. Another pupil can stay with the in-

jured child. If a child or group of children are lost they should have been told to stay where they are. Additional common sense safety tips that can be discussed with children are as follows:

    A.   Always walk; never run,
    B.   Never wander away from the group,
    C.   Never put your hand into a hole or a place that you cannot first see into, and
    D.   Never throw rocks.

Some minor accidents are bound to happen. You should have with you a basic first aid kit and someone with knowledge of how to use it. You should also know if any children have any special medical problems (heart weakness, diabetes, etc.) that would affect their taking part in some outdoor trips. Finally, it is wise to always have two vehicles (such as a school bus and an automobile) while on outings. Thus, one vehicle is always available to transport an injured student to the nearest medical facility without stranding others at the site.

10. Don't forget the real world is full of surprises. You may find an unexpected teaching opportunity or *teachable moment* that may be even better than the one for which you had planned. Don't be so structured in your plans that you don't allow children and yourself the opportunity to capitalize on such unique learning opportunities.

11. Both by your example and discussions before, during, and after outdoor experiences care should be taken not to harm or pollute the environment. This includes such things as:

    A.   Not collecting things unnecessarily. In non-preserve areas a good rule of thumb is only collect when many similar things can be left for others to enjoy.
    B.   Try to avoid walking on plants and animals.
    C.   Move quietly to avoid disturbing wild creatures.
    D.   Never uproot plants.
    E.   Carefully place specimens collected in plastic bags or plastic containers for carrying back to school. Animals or plants that cannot be adequately cared for back in the classroom should be left in their natural environment.
    F.   Turn back logs and stones after searching.
    G.   Always close gates.
    H.   Carry back any trash or food wrappings to designated trash containers.

Follow-Up Activities

As mentioned repeatedly, an experience or activity outdoors should fit into the pupils on-going curriculum, rather than be an isolated event. In most cases a large amount of material, ideas, information, and unanswered questions will be gathered in the outdoors which will require follow-up work back in the classroom. Questions may have been stimulated which can be developed and answered with school and local resources; others may require subsequent outdoor investigations. The important thing is to insure that the best value is gained from subsequent visits by using them to seek out information which cannot be obtained in the classroom.

Individuals or small groups of pupils may have raised questions on their own, so that subsequent outdoor experiences become an individual or small group inquiry. Preparations for such follow-up experiences will involve making sure that pupils have clear ideas of what they will search for, have decided how they will begin and follow-up the task when they arrive, have thought carefully about the apparatus and equipment they may need, and have checked out how to use it.

If children conducted activities outdoors in order to learn specific concepts, such as the *protective coloration* example given in Chapter 2, the classroom follow-up can be of many sorts to help instill and insure understanding of the concept. Children who enjoy outdoor work will wish to share their experiences and this can be the incentive for such follow-up work. This should be personal work, for children will be attracted by different aspects of their experience and they will wish to make use of various materials in expressing their ideas.

Those who have a lot to say or are too young to write much will enjoy using a tape recorder. Others will need paints, crayons, fabrics, modeling clay, construction paper, graph paper, and writing materials. Some children will need longer than others to think about the visit before they are ready to produce anything. Therefore, materials should be freely available in the classroom at all times so that children can fit this work into their daily program whenever it seems right to do so.

Work likely to be produced includes:

1. Tape recordings of conversations, descriptions and early poems.
2. Pictures that can be mounted.
3. Large murals (cooperative efforts).
4. Models in clay.
5. Illustrated books containing factual descriptions (these would contain contributions from all members of the class).
6. Individual illustrated booklets and diaries.
7. Many children could also construct maps, graphs, charts, displays, sketches, paintings and written accounts.

During these follow-up studies the common objective for children in all groups should be presenting the records in ways that will be meaningful to the other children who have not been concerned with that particular topic or mode of expression. This is no easy task, but the attempt to achieve it is one of the most effective ways in which children can consolidate and deepen their own understanding of the work they have done.

When the work of all the groups is on display, class time will be needed for examining results of the study as a whole, listening to group reports and discussion. If the children's work has brought any significant features or relationships to light this is the time for drawing attention to them and considering whether they are present in any other areas the children have studied. Finally parents and other classes can be invited to school to see what has been learned and to find out how many areas of the curriculum can be expressively communicated using both sides of the brain. Parents can also enjoy their own children's efforts to act as guides to this work.

Teaching Techniques

Successful teachers of outdoor as well as indoor education are not only effective planners and managers of curriculum, children, and resources but also effective in utilizing a wide range of teaching behaviors and strategies that help children achieve a variety of learning goals. Such teachers usually possess the following general teaching characteristics:

1. They have established a learning climate in and out of the classroom where there is a high degree of trust and support between themselves and the children and among the children.
2. They understand children's needs and interests, understand childlike behavior, and know how children best learn.
3. They have a great deal of enthusiasm for the learnings they and the children can have in the outdoors. A British outdoor educator indicated that "When a teacher is alive to the opportunities that any moment of the day can present, the beginning will be very simple and spontaneous."[1] At times this enthusiasm must take the form of becoming a "ham"; the ability to enthuse over the common in order to entice children to observe and inquire.
4. They see themselves as resources for the children's learning not as the "fountains of all knowledge." For the resource-type teacher it is easy to say "I don't know what the heck that is either. Let's take it back to the classroom and see if we can find out what it is from the guidebooks."

5. They are flexible and willing to divert lesson plans when more interesting or teachable moments occur.

Specific teaching behaviors which help promote the kind of inquiry-discovery learning characteristic of most of the activities conducted in the outdoors are as follows:

1. *Ask questions that encourage children to think rather than recall facts and the names of things.* Thinking questions can help provide a focus or outline for an investigation and also permit students to find answers or relationships for themselves. Thinking questions are those that usually have more than one possible answer. A few examples of questions and an outline for an investigation of a problem or question that results from these kinds of questions is presented in Diagram 1.

Diagram 1

Key Thinking Questions

Situation—as you walk along the desert with a group of children you stop at a large ant nest on the ground which is surrounded by a circular path of tiny bits of plant debris.

Key Question	*Stages of the Inquiry Problem Solving Process*
What do you observe?	I. Observation of the ant hill
What question does this ant nest raise?	II. Identification of a question or problem
Why do you think there is the ring of debris around the nest?	III. Make a guess, hypothesis or inference.
What do you think caused this?	
Why do you think the ring of debris is there?	
What can you do to check your guess, hypothesis, or inference?	IV. Determine procedures for answering the question or solving the problem.
What evidence can you actually observe that would support one or another of the guesses, etc.?	V. Collect and record data.
What additional evidence do you need in order to decide which is the most logical explanation? Which can you test in the field? How should you proceed?	
Which should you test back in the classroom? What information do you need to gather in the field to take back?	
What instruments are needed to collect other pertinent data or information?	
Can you devise any controlled experiments to test your guess, hypothesis, or inference?	
How do the results, data, or information gathered relate to your guess, hypothesis or inference?	VI. Recheck guess, hypothesis or inference.
What did you find out? What happened in your experiment? If you were to redo the experiment, how would you insure more accurate results?	VII. Make conclusions or start over if necessary.

While all the above key questions and procedures may not be used with all problems or questions and with all ages of children, such an approach can eventually lead children to the excitement of answering questions posed from the environment.

2. *Respond to children's comments and answers in such a way that thinking does not cease.* If a child answers a question that has several possible answers, providing a response that indicates the child is right probably inhibits further thinking about the question. Several researchers have discovered that excessive use of praise or positive reinforcement has the following negative effects on children's learning:[2]

A. Students become more dependent on extrinsic rather than intrinsic rewards.
B. Students develop less confidence in themselves.
C. Students don't get as much involved in inquiry-problem solving or open discovery because they are conditioned for a quick pay off of praise.
D. Students are less likely to share information or listen to other students.
E. Peer teasing of those receiving praise occurs.
F. Praise makes students over-confident and unable to concentrate on complex learning tasks.

When dealing with real questions or problems from the outdoors, like "What causes the rings around certain ant nests?" the answers can usually be found through observation and experimentation. If, however, teachers continually provide right answers students will not have the opportunity to develop their own thinking and problem solving skills. An alternative to giving praise or positive responses is the use of responses which are neutral in interpretation. A *neutral response* is one that indicates you hear and understand the child's response but does not indicate whether the response is right or wrong. Examples of neutral responses are as follows:

I see.	Can you show us?
That's an interesting idea.	Silence.
Thank you.	Smile.
O.K.	Do you agree with Jon?
Repeat the answer.	How could we find out?
Alright.	That's a possibility.
What evidence do you have that . . .	Fine.

While being neutral in responses to children's comments or questions will promote further inquiry, there are perhaps two occasions when answers to questions or solutions to problems can be given.

A. When, in your judgement, the students do not have the know-how or equipment to actually find the answer(s) by themselves. When this occurs, you've probably come upon a question or problem that requires formal logic or abstract thinking to understand and it is probably inappropriate for elementary school children to really understand anyway. Go ahead and tell them the answer or give a short explanation, provided you have one, but don't expect them to truly understand if they aren't able to have a concrete experience with the concept or idea involved.
B. When not knowing the answer could be dangerous. Rather than children discovering what kind of nest a black widow spider lives in or which end of the scorpion does the damage, you're better off telling them directly.

3. *Listen to children.* Encourage them to ask questions, to give explanations, or to express feelings without interrupting with your chatter. If teachers ask too many questions, give too many answers and explanations, and offer too many suggestions, they don't have opportunities to hear

what children are interested in or saying. Also, too much teacher talk interferes with children's opportunity to suggest and try out ideas—in short, to think.

An important aspect of listening is referred to as *wait-time*. This is the pause you allow children after you ask a question and before you call on a child, give an answer, or rephrase the question. It is also the pause you allow a child after a child has made a comment or answered a question.

Diagram 2

Wait Time Pauses

The two important wait times a teacher should consider are shown below:

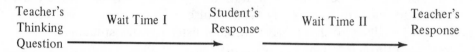

Research indicates most teachers only wait at these two times for only one second or less.[3] However, if thinking questions are being asked and neutral responses are being given then one second is not enough time to formulate answers and think of responses. Research further indicates that if teachers are able to wait at least three seconds students' intellectual development can be enhanced in the following ways:

A. The length of children's responses increases.
B. The appearance of children's speculative thinking (e.g., "It might be the water, but it could also be too many plants") and use of arguments based on evidence begins to occur.
C. Children shift from teacher centered "show and tell" kinds of behavior to child to child dialogues where comparisons of ideas are expressed.
D. Children begin to ask more questions and the number of experiments they need to answer their questions multiplies.[4]

An Overall Teaching-Learning Approach

Much of the emphasis with the teacher characteristics and teaching strategies discussed above relate to the observation, problem identification, and resolution of a problem or question. These processes involve children with the outdoor environment, and while this is the heart of most outdoor education experiences, the time comes when children need to be brought together, usually back in the classroom, to follow-up, to evaluate, and discuss what has gone on and to share results. Finally, if concepts, appreciations, and skills learned are to become part of the children's repetoire, then opportunities also need to be provided to apply these learnings in similar situations.

An overall teaching strategy that incorporates the activity, follow-up, and application learning phases is as follows:

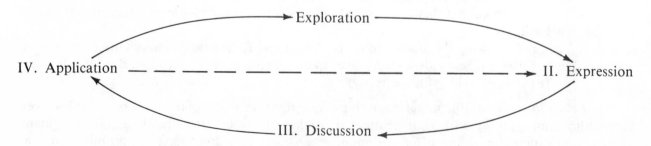

Learning in this sense, provided it is relevent, meaningful, and integrated with the total curriculum, is an on-going process. It is actually cyclical with one learning phase leading to another. Phases of this learning cycle are explained below:

Phase I—Introduction or Exploration

In this phase the concept, process, phenomenon, or persistent problem that is the focus of a unit is introduced. This can be done with a walk or tour of an outdoor site or through a specific indoor or outdoor activity done in the classroom or outdoor site.

The purpose of such activities is to provide children with concrete experiences with the theme topic the children are to learn about. In effect there may be several different activities that are performed, both indoors and outdoors, over any length of time that relate to the concept, process, phenomenon, or problem being investigated. The type of theme category being used for the unit will determine the emphasis of the Introductory activities.

Phase II—Expression of Results; Follow-up Part I

This is the opportunity children need to provide an organization for their learnings and to determine the meanings of their concrete experiences (right brain) in ways that they can communicate to others (left brain). The recent research on left-right brain functions would indicate this is essential in helping to activate both hemispheres of the child's brain to bring about complete understanding and learning. Here children can use any number of modes of expression including mathematics (charts, graphs, formulas), writing (reports, diaries, stories, poems), drama (movement, puppet shows, pantomime), music (instrumental, vocal), art (diorama, mural, models, painting, etc.) and talking (reports, discussions).

Phase III—Discussion; Follow-up Part II

It has been suggested that children don't learn solely by doing but by also thinking about what they have done.[5] Group discussions provide children additional opportunities to share and evaluate learning and for teachers, with the help of reference materials, books, films, and other resource people to help provide mental structures to help children understand and mentally organize the learning resulted from the exploration and expression phases.

The essence of providing mental structures for children is providing labels, definitions, and additional examples of the concepts, processes, phenomenon and problems investigated during the Introduction and Exploration Phase. Unfortunately, many teachers operate under the misunderstanding (prompted by left brain behaviorial psychology) that children should be verbally introduced to the concepts, processes, etc., they are going to learn about before the activities are conducted. Such attempts slow down real understanding of the concepts, processes, etc., because children are forced to use only one side of the brain (the left side) to memorize without first having concrete, first-hand experiences with the concepts, processes, etc. For example in the "create an animal" activity at the end of Chapter 2 the concept of *protective coloration* was the focus of the lesson. Labeling of the concept did not occur until the indoor discussion phase after the child had several experiences creating and finding animals that had been designed with emphasis on their capabilities to blend into the environment. When the concept was labeled it was done using definitions and words drawn from the real experiences the children just had.

Phase IV—Application or Action

Retention of the meaning of a concept, process, phenomenon, or problem may be long lasting if the children are given opportunities to apply their understandings or act upon their problem solving efforts. Children's understanding of *protective coloration,* for example, could be applied in another activity where they are encouraged to create plants designed to be attractive and visible to potential pollunators (the opposite of protective coloration).

If, on the other hand, children are dealing with environmental problems or issues that are real to them there are possibilities of applying the learnings to *action* problem solving. Unfortunately, many teachers and students only reach the point of identifying problems, collecting data, and determining what could be done to resolve the problem. If one goal of education is to help children learn to develop the skills and appreciations of decision making then they should also have the opportunity to learn and utilize these skills in schools. Many classrooms of children have made significant impacts on their environment by acting to help publicize and reduce such problems as traffic congestion near their school, litter on the playground, excessive use of electricity in the school, or in such projects as the saving of land preserves threatened by housing developments, or help in the restoration of historical buildings.

Key steps in action problem solving once the problem has been identified, studied, and researched are as follows:

A. Identify alternative solutions and the implications of each solution. Here implications from an economical, environmental, social and political point of view must be considered, thus incorporating many disciplines.

B. Take action on the basis of the solution(s) selected. Value judgements and trade-offs must be considered in selecting appropriate solutions.

C. Finally, assess the results of the action. Was the desired outcome achieved?

These should be considered the final three steps of the inquiry problem solving process described earlier in Diagram I.

Monitoring Children's Progress and Understandings

Monitoring implies more than formal testing. It also implies that teachers must make continuous assessments about students' progress and understanding, about their interest and motivation, about the appropriateness of the resources and activities selected, and about the success of the teacher's own planning, managing, and teaching behaviors. Monitoring does not normally attempt to isolate and treat differently the outdoor and indoor aspects of the curriculum and learning but should deal with the total learning experiences of children.

Many suggestions have already been provided which relate to the monitoring of how well children are progressing and understanding the "content" of a unit. Such things as art work, projects, diaries, notebooks, and murals are examples which allow teachers an on-going opportunity to evaluate children's accomplishment of some of the goals and objectives of a unit. Children's performance in application activities are another source for monitoring progress and understanding.

Note, the emphasis of these monitoring suggestions is not on formal testing at the end of the unit but on examination of the products of experience and of the processes children use while completing activities. Teacher observations using check sheets and antidocal records are perhaps more useful for monitoring the variety of learning outcomes such as children's use of knowledge, process skills, social skills, attitudes, and interests that were determined to be important by the goals and objectives selected for the unit. Examples of sample check sheets are given in Appendix G.

Formal paper and pencil tests or laboratory tests are useful only to monitor the acquisition of specific facts and skills related to the use of such things as apparatus and mathematical processes. These may be somewhat removed, however, from the actual activity of the students in learning these facts and skills and may provide misleading information if they are the only form of monitoring used.

All this is not to say that the *outdoor aspects* of a school curriculum cannot be measured independently from what occurs in the classroom. Some instruments for evaluating certain results of outdoor education activities have been devised and used by schools. Most are of an opinionnaire-type given to students, teachers, and parents and designed for a specific experience, such as a resident outdoor school. Examples of some are given in Appendix H. These are often helpful in interpreting and justifying a program to the school administration, board of education, and citizens.

Conclusion

This chapter has offered a variety of practical suggestions for planning, managing, carrying out, and monitoring outdoor education experiences with children. A recurrent theme in this whole chapter has been that successful and meaningful outdoor experiences will be those drawn from the existing curriculum and themes. Little justification can be provided for outdoor education experiences which do not do this.

Notes

1. Margaret Collis, *Using the Environment:* part of the Schools Council "Science 5/13 project." (London: MacDonald Educational Ltd., 1974), page 3.
2. Alison Wolf, "Praise and Student Esteem," *Learning Magazine.* Vol. 5, Number 2, October, 1976, pages 24, 26 and 30.
3. Mary Budd Rowe, "Science, Silence, and Sanctions," *Science and Children.* Vol. 6, Number 6, March, 1969.
4. *Ibid.*

Part Two
Activity Suggestions

The second part of this book offers representative activities from the four theme categories identified in Chapter 3 for School Site, Urban, Water, Forest, and Desert Environments. No attempt has been made to present an extensive list of activities because these can be found in the sources reviewed in Chapter 4.

Only basic information for conducting each activity is provided thus leaving it to the teacher to modify activities and add left and right brain emphasis, to accommodate for different grade levels, different size groups, and different environmental conditions. The pages in this part of the book, however, are perforated to allow them to be removed from the book to be used while in the outdoors with children.

Chapter 6

Activities for the School Site

Introduction

The school site has the potential of becoming the most diverse, most provocative, yet least expensive resource for teachers wishing to enhance and enrich their curriculum. Sidewalks, parking lots, grass, flower beds, trees, fences, outside walls, gutters, drainage ditches, and the playground equipment are as much a part of most schools as are libraries, story problems in textbooks and frogs in formaldehyde.

Several suggestions are provided within many of the resources reviewed in Chapter 4 to help in planning and developing a new school site to make it useful as an outdoor laboratory. Suggestions are also given in these sources for modifying and improving existing sites to make them more useful as outdoor learning resources. The scope of this chapter therefore, does not include extensive discussion of how planning and modification might occur. Rather, the intent is to offer a few suggestions for activities that can be done on almost any site. It is hoped you will begin to see additional possibilities on your own as you begin to try some of the following and are encouraged to seek more ideas from the resources cited in Chapter 4.

The activities are placed in four categories representing the four theme categories discussed in Chapter 3: Concept, Process, Phenomenon, and Persistent Problems. Before specific activities are suggested however, the following flow diagram may lead you to some identifying of your own ideas for activities.

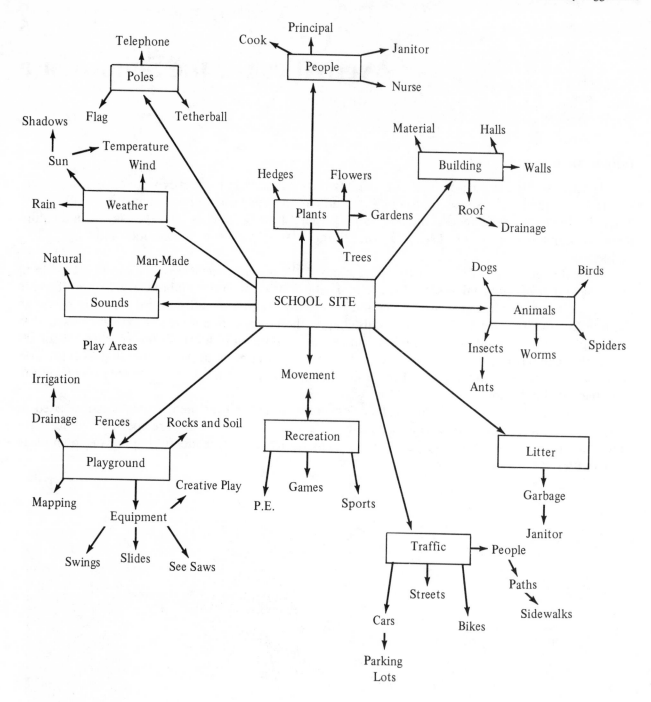

I. **Concepts**

A. *Shadows.* (Requires sunny day.) Designed to provide concrete experiences which lead to understandings of the relationships of the sun, earth and objects on the earth.

1. *Paper Plate Shadows.* (Primary) Give each child a paper plate and have them try the following:

   a. make the roundest paper plate shadow you can.
   b. make the smallest paper plate shadow you can.
   c. make the flattest paper plate shadow you can.
   d. make the tallest and thinnest paper plate shadow you can.
   e. find a partner and place your paper plate shadow on top of your partner's paper plate shadow without the paper plates touching. How far away can the paper plates be and still have their shadows touching?
   f. with the partner and your two paper plates, do anything you want to the paper plates to make some interesting shadows.

2. *People Shadows* (Primary). Provide pairs of students with large sheets of paper and crayons. Have pairs go outside at different intervals to draw each others shadows while standing in a designated spot. The time of day that the shadow was drawn should be identified on the back of the paper. If possible, these drawings should be repeated at three different times during the day. The drawings should be brought and hung in the classroom. Classmates can guess at which time of the day each shadow was made.

3. *X and Your Finger Shadow* (Primary).

   a. Draw an X on the sidewalk or paved surface.
   b. Touch the X with your finger's shadow. Begin by having your hand close to the ground.

When a child finally figures out where the finger needs to be placed to keep it's shadow on the "X," the delight of the discovery can be seen on the child's face.

    c.   See how far away from the spot you can move your finger and still keep your finger's shadow on the X.

    d.   Stand back from someone else's X. Can you guess where to place your finger to have your finger's shadow hit that spot? Try it.

4. *Shadow Tag* (Primary). Shadow tag is like other kinds of tag where one person is "IT" and tries to catch others to make them "IT." Try some of the following ways to play tag using shadows:

    a.   the person who is "IT" tries to catch others by touching their shadow with his foot.

    b.   the person who is "IT" tries to catch others by touching their shadow with his shadow.

    c.   the person who is "IT" tries to catch others by touching their shadow with his hand's shadow.

Like other tag games there are places that are "FREE" and "SAFE." In shadow tag these would be places where your shadow cannot be caught. Where might some of these places be?

Try playing this game at different times during the day (9:00 A.M., Noon, 3:00 P.M.).

Would it be easier to be "IT" in the morning, noon or afternoon?

5. *Shadow Clocks* (Intermediate). Provide each group of three to five students with a large square piece of butcher paper, a lump of clay, a drinking straw and a ruler. They should go outside and complete the following tasks:

    a.   place the piece of butcher paper on the ground in a sunny spot.

    b.   place a small piece of clay at the center of the paper.

    c.   put the staw into the clay so that it is held straight up.

    d.   trace the shadow made by the straw on the paper.

    e.   measure the shadow and record the length. Record the time on the sheet of paper next to the shadow line.

    f.   repeat the same procedure in 15 minutes.

    g.   what happens to the shadow length as the day goes on?

    h.   where would a 12:00 o'clock shadow have been?

    i.   where will a 4:00 P.M. shadow be?

    Follow-up. Discuss—if you leave the shadow clock where it is will it work tomorrow as well as it does now? Will it work as well in one week?

    Investigate other methods of telling time using shadows.

6. *Sun Fan* (Intermediate). Provide groups of children with a lump of clay and four or five drinking straws and have them complete the following:

    a.   stick a long lump of clay on a sunny spot on the ground.

    b.   now stick a drinking straw into the clay. Place it so that it does not cast a shadow. Where must it point to have no shadow?

    c.   fifteen minutes later see if the straw casts a shadow. Does the straw still point directly to the sun? How can you explain what you observe?

    d.   then stick a second straw into the clay. Point it toward the sun so that it casts no shadow. Be careful not to move the first straw.

    e.   in this way add a new straw every 15 minutes. The straws will show how the sun seems to change its position in the sky.

B. *Change.* (Living things grow and change, there is natural and manmade change in the environment.)

    1. *Living and Nonliving* (Primary). There are many things in the environment. Some are living and some are not. Living things grow and change. They make more living things and they can die. For a young child to begin to understand the interactions between man and his environment he should first understand the basic differences between living and nonliving things.

    Take the students to the school site and have them find five living things. Show them to a friend. Now find three nonliving things. Discuss differences between living and nonliving things.

    Have students bring the three nonliving things back to the classroom. Give each group of students three seeds and have them plant them and the 3 nonliving things. Water all six. Keep a record. What happens? How are living things different?

    While you are waiting for something to happen with the planted items have students look for other nonliving things in the school. Make rubbings of them using crayon, chalk or pencil. Compare the rubbings with the objects from day to day. Do nonliving things change?

    2. *Outdoor Photography* (Intermediate and Upper Grades). Provide students with Polaroid cameras and give them any of the following challenges:

    a. photograph evidence that a natural change is occurring on the school site.

    b. take two pictures—one of which is responsible for a change in the other.

    c. go outside and take a series of three pictures so the first causes a change in the second, the second related to the third, but so the last picture appears to have no connection to the first picture taken.

    d. have a student take two random photographs of the outdoor environment and have the rest of the class tell a story about both pictures.

    e. other—you invent one.

    Once the photographs are taken, a discussion can be held which focuses on the nature of change. Short term? Long term? Natural? Man-made? What is the effect of these changes on the environment?

C. *The Environment.* (Consisting of the natural [living and nonliving] and man-made aspects and their interrelationships.)

1. *Animal Habitats* (Intermediate). Use this as an exploration activity. Take the class as a whole or in groups of ten, but work in groups of three to five to explore as many places (environments or habitats) as they can. Have them look for any signs of animals or actual animal life. They do not have to be identified, just found. Evidence of animal life could include sounds, partly eaten foods, droppings, homes, nests, feathers, holes in ground, logs or trees, spider webs, teethmarks, egg cases, tracks, etc.

   When returning to classroom have students plot their findings on a map of the school site. This can lead to follow-up activities regarding the environmental factors such as light, moisture, temperature, wind, presence of plants, etc., that account for the presence or lack of animals in each habitat.

2. *School Yard Safari* (Intermediate). This makes a good right brain follow-up to the previous activity. Ask students to take a "pretend" safari onto the school site. "Pretend" that buildings are mountains and great rocks. Look into the nooks and crannies for living things. Are the shrubs similar to the undergrowth of a jungle? Look for signs of life there as well.

   Are the trees just like some in the jungle? Search them for wild things such as insect eggs, capsules, spider webs, leaves that have been nibbled.

   Go looking for live animals to "capture" beneath your hand lens.

3. *Miniforest* (Primary). Even an arm-circle of grass can provide a model of the environment of a forest. Take the children to a grassy spot on the school site and have everyone lie on the ground face down. Each should make an arm circle by stretching arms out in front of them on the ground. Some of the possible things to do are:

   a. find at least five different plants inside the arm circle.
   b. see if they can find any tiny animals crawling through the grass.
   c. what else can be seen? (Any dead leaves or twigs?)
   d. spread the grass apart and describe what is seen.

   Follow-up activity such as art work, drama or creative writing should emphasize the point that plants and animals live together in an environment.

One only has to observe carefully a small bit of grass to discover the world of a "Miniforest."

4. *Opposites Hunt* (Upper). Provide students with a map of the school site or a designated portion of the school site and ask the students to predict and indicate on their maps where they think the following will be found:

   a. warmest place and the coolest place.
   b. wettest place and the driest place.
   c. windiest place and the calmest place.
   d. brightest place and the darkest place.

   Next provide groups of three to five students with necessary equipment (thermometer, wind gauge, radiometer and dampness paper) to find the above variables. They can place their actual findings on the map.

   When complete, bring all groups together to discuss findings. How good were their predictions? Will they predict these conditions will remain the same during the entire day, week, month, year? Do any of the extremes of the variables recorded on the map seem to relate to each other; i.e., do the coolest places seem also to be the darkest, etc.? In what ways does man affect microenvironments?

5. *An Environment Through Whose Eyes* (Intermediate/Upper). This is another right brain activity to do after study of a particular microenvironment of the school site. Have students choose one of the members of the environment (a plant or animal). A discussion should be held about how this member is interrelated with other living and nonliving aspects of the environment (including the activities of man).

   Then have students write a story through the eyes of that member, indicating what is happening to the environment and what the environment will be like in the future. These can then be read to the class.

   Follow-up discussion could deal with such things as: is the environment you studied protected? Are new laws needed? Who should be responsible for protecting it? Predict what will happen in your environment if one of the living things disappeared; if one of the nonliving factors changed greatly.

   Dramas could then be put on with some of the stories.

6. *Welcome to the Environment* (Primary). Before young children can begin to appreciate the role of man in the environment, they need to understand what the environment is. Start the definition by action. Take the students for a walk around the school. Have the students listen, smell, touch things around them. Taste (where appropriate). Talk about the things you observe. The many things around make up the environment. We all live in the environment.

   To go beyond the definition level it would be easy to get to the values level after this short trip. Continue with these questions and activities:

   a. what things do you like in the environment? Make a collage or painting that shows the things you like.
   b. what things would you change? Make a list. Tell why each should be changed.
   c. write a poem or story about your environment. Read it to the class.
   d. draw a fish. Draw the things you would find around it. This is the fish's environment. Is it the same as ours?
   e. does everyone have the same environment? What makes an environment good?

7. *Feelings About the Environment* (Primary). To begin to help children appreciate the environment, it is helpful to place them in situations where they have to make value judgments. Start by asking children what makes them happy. Have them find a picture from a book or magazine of one thing that makes them happy and explain why it makes them happy.

Then have them find a picture of something that makes them feel sad and explain this to a classmate.

Next have pictures of various aspects from the environment and ask, "How do you feel when you see . . . (such things as) . . . rain? litter? fire? a dead animal?"

Follow this up by having the students act out or write about: what makes a hungry animal happy? What makes a thirsty animal happy?

Follow-up questions might be: what things do animals need? What do plants need? How are we like plants? How are we like animals?

Finally, everyone should do something to make someone happy. How did you do it?

D. *Energy.* Several basic activities can be done using the school site to give students experience with a variety of forms of energy. These would only be appropriate for intermediate and upper grades. Sample idea starters are as follows:

1. *Energy Collage.* Have students collect pictures of energy users and energy sources. Groups of three to five students can make a collage of their pictures. This will provide you an idea of student's understanding of energy sources.

2. *Solar Energy.* Put a jar of water in the sun. Measure the temperature. Wait an hour. Measure again. What happened? What was the source of energy?

3. *Make a Pin Wheel.* Blow on it. What happens? How is this like a windmill? What was the source of energy?

4. *Energy Home Survey.* List all the ways energy is used in the home. Have a family meeting to share your survey. Plan ways to save energy. Try it. Keep records. Did your family cut down on energy consumption?

5. *Energy School Survey.* List all the energy users in the school and the kind of energy they use. Determine how energy can be saved. Make a list of suggestions. Meet with your principal. Ask him to help you. Try some of the suggestions.

II. **Processes**

    A. *Observation Skills.*

        1. *Scavenger Hunt* (Any Grade Level). This popular activity is an excellent way to give children an opportunity to explore a new area in a short period of time as well as develop observation skills and imagination. Have the class divide into teams of about five students and give each group a list of things that could be found in the school environment. Encourage children to use their imaginations on some of the items. After all, things always are not what they seem to be. An example of the things children could look for are as follows (the list could be adjusted for different grade levels):

           a. a square in nature
           b. a seed
           c. candy wrapper
           d. broken eggshell
           e. broken potato chip
           f. evidence of animal life
           g. the red C (imagination required)
           h. a feather
           i. an insect gall
           j. a grass hopper (not grasshopper—requires imagination)
           k. evidence of man
           l. a circle in nature
           m. a smooth rock
           n. a hairy leaf
           o. one of nature's tools (imagination)
           p. a piece of string
           q. a piece of glass
           r. something bumpy
           s. something cool
           t. a bird's song
           u. something inconspicuous
           v. something sculpted
           w. something absorbent

        One important footnote: this is a good activity to begin to instill the idea that activities can be done in the outdoors that do not harm the environment. Emphasis should be placed on taking things that improve the quality of life (removing litter and glass) and not taking such things as a circle in nature that may be part of something living.

        A follow-up discussion can focus on the differences and similiarities in the objects found.

        2. *Sense Walk* (Any Grade Level). This activity works best with a group of no more than 12 students but can be attempted with a whole class if necessary. Take the children for a walk on the school site or neighborhood. Once outside find a particular spot with the group where you can either stand or sit away from other students. Then ask the students to close their eyes, and without talking concentrate on the sounds around them. Discuss the sounds heard and the feelings each sound produces.

        Begin the walk again and have the students be aware of the smells around them for three minutes. Smell leaves and trunks of trees, the air, flowers, objects found, car engines, etc. Discuss the smells found.

Continue the walk having students touch everything around them as if they were touching them for the first time. Stop after three minutes, and discuss how different things felt.

In the next three minutes, see everything around you as if for the first time.

Finally, find another place to sit down and have students close their eyes. Spend the next three minutes on taste—for example, chew some gum, eat a piece of candy or an apple—something you really like.

Complete the walk back to the classroom, keeping sense activity in the foreground. Allow yourself and encourage the students to experience whatever presents itself.

An excellent language arts follow-up to this activity is to have children list all the sense words they used in their discussions while outdoors. Sense words for hearing, smelling, feeling, tasting and seeing can be categorized. These then can be used to create stories or poems.

3. *Other Sense Walks* (Primary). Sense walks can also be spent on each individual sense; i.e., "sound hike," "touch and feel hike," "color hike" which are similar to the above. The emphasis can be on feelings; i.e., which sounds do you like? Why? What colors do you think the sound of a truck has? Language development can also be emphasized; i.e., find the *hariest* leaf, *softest* leaf, *smoothest* rock, and find something bumpy.

4. *A Rock Experience* (Intermediate to Upper). This activity is designed to sensitize and help develop right brain qualities. Each child is to find a fist-size rock. From here it works better to have each student find a spot on the site where he/she can be alone. They should then complete the following directions (which can be written out for each child):

   a.   hold the rock in your hand.
   b.   look at the rock. See its shape, color(s), ridges and indentations.
   c.   feel the weight of the rock.
   d.   toss it up and down in your hand.
   e.   feel the texture of all the surfaces of the rock.
   f.   squeeze it and find out how hard it is.
   g.   close your eyes and hold the rock against your cheek, chin and forehead.
   h.   experience its temperature, its texture.
   i.   allow the rock to settle gently over one of your eyelids. Hold it there for 30 seconds and then take it away.
   j.   experience that eye.
   k.   put your lips against the rock. Experience its temperature, texture, taste, and smell.
   l.   let your rock rest on top of your head.
   m.   leave it there 30 seconds to one minute. Experience its weight.
   n.   take the rock off and experience how you feel.
   o.   open your eyes and again see the rock.
   p.   return to the classroom.

A good follow-up to this activity is to have students discuss their experience in groups of five students, thus allowing more to talk than might normally talk in a large group discussion. By the way, this is one you should try with the children as well. If the students see and know you will try something risky, they will try it as well.

5. *Observe and sketch* (Intermediate and Upper). Find two trees with different shapes. Observe and sketch each, one tree at a time. Here are some helpful suggestions for

novice "artists"; emphasis is on observation techniques, not artistic quality. The results may be surprising, however.

a. Look at the tree from a distance.

b. With your finger, "trace" (in the air) the shape of the tree. Do this from the ground up and from top down to the ground.

c. Describe the shape of the tree to others in your group.

d. Make a "telescope" with your hands. Look through this "telescope" at your tree from a distance.

e. Describe how the branches go out from the trunk (up, out, down?).

f. Hold out your arms to show how the branches grow out from the tree trunk.

g. Go closer to the tree. What else do you notice about it?

h. Get close to the trunk of the tree. Look up into the tree. What do you see?

i. Go to a comfortable place where you can see your tree. Sketch it with a crayon you brought along, keeping in mind the things already discovered about shape, branches, and other important observations.

j. Repeat with a second tree.

6. *Looking for Opposites Outdoors* (Any Grade Level). This is an excellent left brain language development activity that can lead to a right brain experience with one form of poetry.

    While the children are indoors, ask them to list five pairs of opposite words on paper. Such things as up-down, hot-cold, happy-sad, are examples.

    Then have the students go out on the school site, and look for examples to match each pair of opposite words. You will find that children will create many pairs of words that have something to do with the classroom such as ceiling-floor, front-back, boy-girl, inside-outside. In such cases children should be encouraged to use their imaginations (actually trying to form metaphors or similies) to find appropriate examples.

    Children again can be reminded they do not have to actually bring back examples (where this will be harmful to the environment and living things in it); rather just locate where these occur. Once complete, a discussion can be conducted wherein children describe some of the "interesting" opposites they found outdoors. Opposites for which no examples could be found by individuals can be discussed by the whole group to allow others to think of (right brain style) matches.

    Upon return to the classroom the form of poetry called *Diamante* can be described for older children and one of the pairs of opposites used to start and end the poem. This form of poetry is described in the next chapter.

    For younger children lists can be made of the opposites used along with a description or display of the "things" found to represent these opposites. Children are thus acquiring many experiences and examples of what different words mean to different people.

B.   *Measuring and Estimating.*

1.   *Nonstandard Units* (Primary). The following represent measurement activities that can occur in the outdoors using nonstandard units. These should be used with primary children to help give them the idea that units are man-made and eventually to a better understanding of the concept of meter or yard.

a.   *Measuring With Body Parts.* How many different ways can you use your body to measure? (Fingers, hands, body length, arm span, etc.) Record the findings.

Now go to the school site and measure the width of the basketball court using all the ways you mentioned. Were some of the units hard (impractical) to use? Why? Which were easier to use?

Now measure the height of a blade of grass. Which units were most practical?

Did everyone get the same results? Why or why not? This could lend to the necessity of having a standard unit such as Bobbie's height or Sarah's finger, etc. Perhaps a stick the height of Bobbie or a strip of paper the size of Sarah's finger could be used instead of having to use Bobbie and Sarah all the time.

b.   *Measuring with String, Sticks and Wheels.* Long distances measured in quantitative units mean little to young children. The physical act of measuring sometimes helps build necessary understandings.

Use a ball of string or some ticker tape to measure the length of a portion of the school building. Now measure the width of the basketball court. Can you tell at a glance which is the longer distance? The two lengths of string can be laid out together to determine the longest.

While some children find string satisfactory for measuring and comparing longer distances, others may prefer to use sticks or wheels. Sticks such as paper clips, broom handles, yardsticks, meter sticks (the latter two need not be defined as standard units—they are just sticks at this point) or wheels (such as bicycle or trundle) can be used. Everytime the wheel makes one complete turn while rolling on the ground, that represents "one wheel" distance (actually a straightened out version of the circumference of the wheel).

In their first attempts to measure distance using sticks, children often construct an actual line of "sticks" from one point to another. If they run out of sticks before reaching their goal, someone may suggest reusing a few of the first sticks in the line. Eventually children will think of using a single stick over and over again to finish the job.

Have the children choose from the following to measure some predetermined distances on the school site (paper clip, broom stick, ruler, straw, meter stick).

2.   *Kilometer Walk* (Any Grade Level). If you were asked "what is a mile?" you would probably come up with definitions such as 5,280 feet, 1760 yards, four times around the 1/4 mile track, 14 laps of the pool, or distance between major street exits on the expressway. Of these, which has the most meaning for you? Your answer is probably not the first two. Why? Because any of the latter have some kind of emotional attachment based on concrete experiences with the distance of a mile. While knowing a mile has 5,280 feet may be part of the verbal definition it does not help one truly understand the "concept" of mile. Understanding requires both the right and the left brain.

Now that the metric system is upon us we can better help children learn the system by providing as many emotional experiences with the different units as possible. Try this to help build a real (not a verbal) definition of kilometer.

Tell the children that after lunch they are going on a Kilometer Walk to help them digest their food. Show the children a Meter Trundle Wheel and have them see that everytime the wheel goes around (and there is a click on some) this represents one meter and that there are 1,000 meters in a kilometer (verbal definition that probably has no meaning). You should have alerted the rest of the staff that you are doing this as well and indicate they may join in if they wish.

Have the students line up and begin walking with the wheel and counting out loud as you walk. Different children can carry signs that say 25 meters, 50 meters, 100 meters, etc.—enough for each child. As that mark is reached, they hold up their sign. This helps everyone keep track of how far you have gone. As you walk you can begin to weave in and out of different classrooms, asking others to join the line if they would like. Go by the principal's office and ask them to join as well. Eventually lead outdoors and around the neighborhood and playground. Plan to end your trip somewhere in a shady comfortable spot on the school site. Perhaps refreshments could be waiting for you.

As you are sitting around resting up discuss with the children how it felt to walk a kilometer. Back inside the children will be eager to write about their walk. Encourage them to emphasize the feelings they had.

3. *Techniques for Estimating and Measuring Height and Distance.* (Intermediate and Upper Grades) The following activities are designed to give you examples of the variety of techniques that can be used in measuring height and distance. Try out and compare the various methods on different heights and distances. Perhaps you can devise methods or modifications of your own.

   a. *Estimation.* Ask a friend of known height to stand underneath a tree or tall object. From your standpoint estimate how many times your friend would fit into the tree's height. Calculate in feet.

      Repeat using a pencil held vertically at arm's length to estimate the tree's height.

   b. *"As High As It Is Far."* Material: Thumbtack with plumbline right angled to isosceles triangle of cardboard.

      Move until you can sight the top of the tree along the sloping edge of the triangle. Keep the upright edge vertical using the plumbline. Measure the distance from the tree. Add your eye height to give you the tree's height.

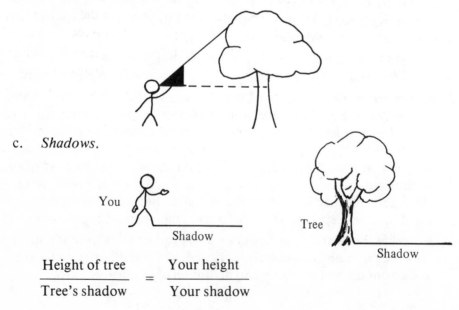

   c. *Shadows.*

You

Shadow

Tree

Shadow

$$\frac{\text{Height of tree}}{\text{Tree's shadow}} = \frac{\text{Your height}}{\text{Your shadow}}$$

Measure your height. _____   Your shadow. _____

Tree's shadow. _____   Calculate and record the tree's height.

d. *Hypsometer*. Material: hypsometer, measuring device. Directions: The string AL establishes a vertical line. How would you hold your hypsometer so that you know the soda straw is level? This gives you a way of locating a point P on the building (or whatever tall thing you are trying to measure) that is level with point A. Measure the distance AP.

By sighting at point 0, string AL automatically forms a collection of triangles (ABC, AB'C', AB"C") with the edge of your hypsometer that are similar to triangle APO. Is AP in triangle APO proportional to AB" in triangle AB"C"? Using the graph paper attached to the hypsometer, can you devise a suitable scale to figure out the distance PO?

Is PO the height of the building? What is the height of the building (or object you are trying to measure)?

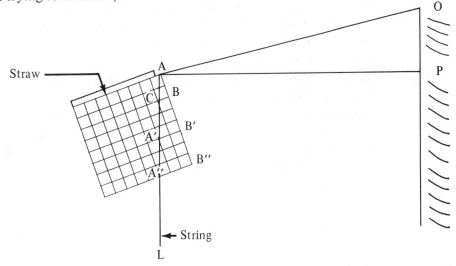

e. *Estimate Short Distances*. To estimate short distances, use the boy scout method. Take a position away from the tree (etc.). With one eye closed and arm outstretched, cover the tree with your thumb. Close your other eye and open the first. Estimate the distance (level with the tree) between the first and second position of your thumb. Multiply this distance by ten to obtain the distance of the tree.

Repeat using two other positions and find the average of your results. How does this work? Look for similar triangles to help you figure this out.

f. *Measuring Longer Distance*. Select an object like a tree that is some distance away. Using a scale drawing, distances can be determined using a known base and two angles. Take a reading of angles X and P for your data.

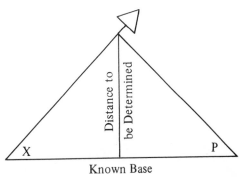

4. *Faster than a Speeding Ant* (Intermediate and Upper). Find a place where ants are active (actually any small animal such as a cricket or pillbug can be used). Notice how fast they travel. Allow the children to determine a method of measuring the speed. Here is one possible way. Children can trace the path of an ant on the sidewalk with a piece of chalk. Another student measures off a time interval; i.e., 10 seconds, 30 seconds, 1 minute. A string is then laid on the chalk track. When straightened out the length of string then represents the distance the insect traveled in the given amount of time. Have children figure out the rate of speed of the insect; i.e., feet per second, miles per hour, meters/hour. How many different ways can the rate of speed be represented?

Children can invent other unique ways of measuring distance by providing such equipment as rulers and straws.

5. *Measuring the Speed of a Car* (Upper). This is a good followup for the above activity because the same basic procedures can be applied. Have students identify two markers that are along side the road. These can be such things as telephone poles, trees, fire hydrants or stakes placed just for this purpose. The distance between markers should be measured. Then, as students stand on the playground, they can time with a stop watch the time it takes a car to pass by the two markers. The rate of speed can then be determined.

Using knowledge of the posted speed limit the students can determine whether any cars may be violating the speed limit. In an actual case, using this procedure over many days, the students discovered one car repeatedly "broke the speed limit," according to their method at about the same time every day. They got the car's license number and reported this to the police. Shortly thereafter, the police set up radar procedures and caught the violator.

C. *Counting* (Number Experiences for Primary Grades). Examples of the kinds of activities that can be done are as follows:

1. Find one of something in your area. Find 10 of something. Go up as high as the children are able; i.e., find 100 of something, find 1,000 of something, then find a 1,000,000 of something. How can you prove the number of each you have?

Estimation can be used here as well.

2. In associating numerals one through nine, with corresponding sets, take a walk around the outside of the school. Stop at different places for children to draw or observe:

1 flagpole	9 bicycles
2 trees	3 swings
1 fire hydrant	4 teetertotters

3. *Zero—The Number of an Empty Set.* How many trees in one section of lawn? How many elephants in one section of playground? How many cars in one section of lawn?

D. *Classification.* This is a process that requires observation of properties of various objects. On and near the school several living and nonliving objects can be classified by children. By doing the following activity, children discover that all standard classification systems are man-made. Follow-up work for each activity could involve using keys for identifying names of objects which are really systems of agreed upon classification models that were also developed by people somewhere to make communication easier.

1. *Invent a Tree Classification System* (Intermediate Grades). This focuses on the development of a binary (two groups) system of classification. Take the children to the school site and ask them to make careful observation of the trees. Have the students determine two major groups. Each group should have some characteristics that the other group does not have. Example: those with spines and those without spines if there are cactus. There should be at least two specimens in each group.

   Once you have formed two groups, try to subdivide each into two more groups, using other prominent characteristics. Be sure students have a good reason for this new grouping.

   Repeat the process but this time select different characteristics for your grouping. For each new subgroup be sure the students describe the characteristics used to distinguish the new group. If different groups of children have been working on the same task, they can compare their groupings. Did any of them use the same characteristics to determine groups?

   An example of the system for 9 trees might be as follows:

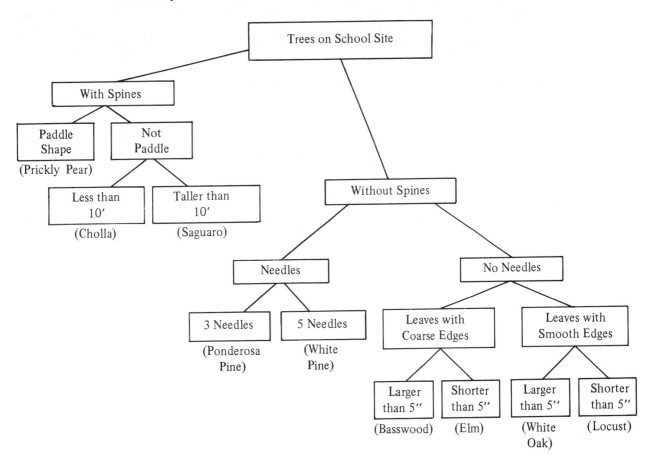

Consider the following: how many ways are there to classify a given collection of organisms? How many subgroups can be made from a given collection? What is the smallest number that can be in a group? Are there certain characteristics that can be used to group any collection of living things?

2. *Classifying Low Plants* (Primary). Have children:

   a. count and record the different kinds of plants in a given area they can find that grow below their knees.

   b. develop a system of classifying those that have few leaves, have many leaves, have stickers, have flowers.

3. *Classifying High Plants* (Primary). Do the same as above with those plants that grow above the children's knees.

Follow-up activities for these two primary activities could involve language arts; write a riddle about one of the plants using properties observed. Example:

   What plant grows below your knees?
   Has many leaves?
   Has stickers and has a white flower?

Or, write an imaginary story explaining how the tallest weed became so tall.

4. *Classifying Nonliving Objects* (Intermediate). A common source of classification is rocks. Many books are available to suggest ideas and techniques. (Rocks and charts from *Elementary Science Study* is a good one.) Do not overlook those things not often classified, however, such as:

   a. houses in the neighborhood; shape, roof shape, type and materials in construction.

   b. fences or walls; types, materials, height.

   c. nonhousing structures; type, function.

   d. bicycles; size, shape, gears, brakes.

   e. automobiles; size, horsepower, foreign or domestic.

III. **Phenomenon**

A. *Playground Equipment.* Most pieces of playground equipment work on the basis of scientific principles, thus a study of equipment can be integrated with many science and mathematical concepts and skills.

1. *Tetherball Pole and Basic Astronomy* (Upper Grades). The ancient astronomers did not have any telescopes. They used a simple device—a vertical pole called a *gnome*. They also laid out an east-west line and marked out a scale to record the point on the horizon where heavenly objects set.

   With this equipment they discovered many basic facts. They found the length of the year and the tilt of the Earth's axis. Using the sun, they determined when noon occurred. The early astronomers were even able to predict eclipses of the sun and moon.

   You and your children can duplicate some of their observations. You will need a tetherball pole that rarely is in shadows, a protractor devise, graph paper, and a measuring device.

The tetherball pole provides an excellent school yard astronomical sighting device.

What to do. The suggestions below serve as ideas to be carried out over a long period of time and at different times of the day. Accomplish what you can.

The tetherball pole is your only astronomical instrument. You sight from it to see where the moon, stars, and planets rise and set. You measure the shadow of the pole to study the sun.

a. Start out by measuring the shadow of the pole at regular intervals during one day. Near noon, measure every 15 minutes. Record the date, time, and shadow length. Indicate the time of the shortest shadow. Construct a graph to keep track of your readings.

b. A line drawn from the bottom of the pole to the tip of this shortest shadow gives you a north-south line. Several days of observation will increase the accuracy of this line.

c. What happens to the shadow length as the day goes on? Why is the time of the shortest shadow not always noon by the clock? (Think of standard time, daylight time, and possible other effects.)

d. Repeat these measurements as often as you can during the year. Be sure to get good readings late in the month of December and late in June.

e. Each day, on a graph, plot your shortest shadow against day of the year. Report to the class what the graph shows. Indicate the connection with the seasons. How can you use this graph to measure the length of the year?

f. Now make a diagram *to scale* like the following. Draw the vertical pole. Draw the shortest daily shadow recorded. Draw the longest noon shadow recorded. Draw a line from the top of the pole to each shadow tip.

g. Use a protractor to carefully measure angles A and B. Now subtract the smaller angle from the larger. Then divide by two. You have just found the amount the Earth's axis is tilted. Confirm this from drawings in your science book.

h. Follow the diagram and divide the angle at the pole top in half. Draw the line down to make angle C. Subtract this angle from 90° and you have found the latitude of your observatory.

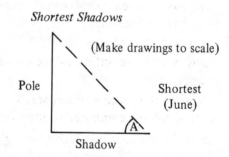

Shortest Shadows

(Make drawings to scale)

Pole   Shortest (June)

Shadow

Longest Shadows

Pole   Longest (December)

Shadow

Also find $\dfrac{A - B}{2}$ = tilt of Earth's axis.

Also, find value halfway between A and B. Call this C.

$$90° - C = \text{latitude of observatory}$$

Other Observations that can be made are as follows:

i.   Using a pole and the sun's shadow, you have already found the length of the year, the tilt of the Earth's axis, and your latitude. The moon and stars cast no shadows so they must be observed by another ancient method. You observe where they set from night to night. Lay out an east-west line from your pole using right-angled triangles, or use a compass or paint.

Put up a marker for the east and west points. Add some kind of scale, perhaps chalk marks every foot on either side. See illustration.

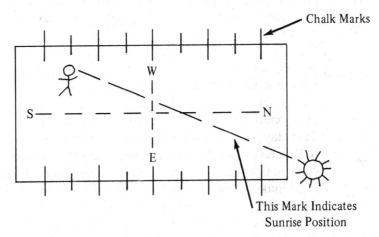

Chalk Marks

This Mark Indicates
Sunrise Position

j.   Record where the sun sets each day. Does it always set due west? Is there any connection between the setting point and the length of the shadow for that day? Or with the Season?

k.   Find out if the moon behaves like the sun. Measure its setting (or rising) several weeks in a row. (Newspapers often give rising and setting times). How does its setting direction differ from that of the sun in amount of change per day? What is its phase when it sets closest to the sun? Does the setting point of the full moon differ from the setting point of the sun on the same day? You will find the answer varies with the season of the year.

How would the setting of the moon agree with the setting of the sun six months from now?

l.   Measure the place a bright star sets for several weeks. How does a star or moon setting behave compared to the sun?

Stand in one spot north of your pole. Record the times a bright star passes across the pole. Do this several nights in a row, standing on the same spot. What is the time difference from night to night? On the basis of your figures, determine when the star will pass the pole six months from now. What problems would you have in observing such a crossing?

Excellent follow up investigations within the social studies could be with some of the ancient astronomy devices such as Stonehenge in England. In Arizona the "big house" or Casa Grande may also have been a sighting device.

2. *Swings and the Pendulum Principle* (Intermediate and Upper). Everything you do is influenced by gravity. If gravity stopped, so would all the pendulum clocks. Maybe worse, all the teetertotters and the swings on the playground would no longer work. On the playground you can learn about the science of swinging and falling bodies.

Have one of your students swing into a high arc on one of the swings and then coast to a stop. Find some answers to the following questions.

Observations:

a.   Does the swing move faster when it is going high as compared to when it is almost stopped?

b.   Is the time of a swing different when it is going high? To measure this, count the number of times the swing comes closest to the ground in ten seconds. What did you find?

   The *period* of the swing is used as a standard of measurement. A period is the time of one complete backward and forward swing. Check the time between two consecutive passes of the lowest part of the forward motion. For more accuracy, time five to ten periods in a row and get an average.

c.   Put two people safely on the swing. What do you find out about the period of the swing now? Persuade a heavy child or adult to let you time his swing period. Time an empty swing, and one with a heavy book. Make a graph. Along the bottom, mark off a scale for the swing period. Along the side, mark off a scale for weight. Put a dot on the proper place of the graph for each separate measurement you have made. Now look at the points. What do they suggest about the effects of weight on the length of the swing period?

   Find a swing with much shorter chains than the one you first used. Repeat all your observations. Plot them on the same graph. What does the new data suggest? Think of other ways in which you can measure the effects that length and weight have on the period of a swinging body.

d.   When a swing is at the top of its arc, it actually stops for a moment. The rider is in a weightless state for an instant, just as the astronauts are when orbiting the Earth. This is because the source of the energy (push) of the swing at this point just balances the pull of gravity. If there were no gravity, what would happen? When gravity pulls the swing down, its energy is stored in the weight and the seat. This energy is used in the next upswing. The same thing happens in the seesaw.

e.   What similarity do you find between a child's swing and a pendulum clock? How would you use a teeter-totter design to build a clock? What would happen to a pendulum clock carried on a spaceship into orbit? Why does a swing come to a stop unless it is pumped or pushed?

3.   *Seesaw* (Primary and Intermediate). Children who have enjoyed the seesaw can be encouraged to think about the way it can be affected by different pairs of children. Which children always make one end move downwards? Which children can keep the seat level when they sit in similar places? Which children can keep the seat level by sitting in different places? Can a small light child find a way of raising a heavy child?

   Here children are really playing with a lever which is a bar arranged so that it can be turned about a point or pivot. *Fulcrum* is another name for the pivot. This arrangement can be varied in many ways. Children can also be encouraged to collect examples of the many ways levers are used in everyday life.

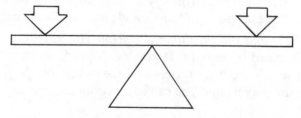

B. *The Playground*. Most playgrounds can be improved to enhance their function as an outdoor laboratory and play area for children. While whole books are written on this topic, the following are offered as a few suggestions for school site development.

1. *Children's Drawings* (Any grade level). If you are going to make an effort to improve the school site, many people should be involved in the planning. One group that should not be left out is the children. One way of ascertaining children's ideas is to ask them to make drawings of what they wished their playground looked like. These pictures can then be analyzed for their basic elements: the frequency of water in the scenes, for example, may indicate the need for ponds or water play areas.

   If children identify places where they can "be off by themselves" then consideration should be given to the development of quiet—private areas. Other clues for change from the drawings may include trees, hills, boulders, buildings or even fires. Frequently there will be a wide range of scale in the drawings; intimate hiding places to massive towers.

2. *Minibeast Sanctuary* (Any Grade Level). Children can locate an unused area and surround it with a low wall of bricks. Various kinds of grass, weeds, clover, and bulbs can be planted to make a herb layer in the enclosed area. Shrubs such as hazel, laurel and hawthorn can then be planted. Finally, birch and citrus trees will eventually make a tree layer. A whole variety of insects, spiders, worms and birds will soon infest the area. Children can sit on the wall and reach into the garden for creatures they want to study.

3. *Planting a Garden* (Any Grade Level). Other books describe the ins and outs of school gardens. Children learn a great deal about plant life cycles, and care and maintenance by having a garden. Harvesting crops such as vegetables and berries is always enjoyable and can lead to a variety of eating ceremonies.

4. *Wall Murals and Black Top Paintings* (Any Grade Level). The school and site can be made more childlike and attractive with the use of children's creative ideas and paint. Outdoor wall murals can become excellent teaching aides; i.e., painting the alphabet, the numerals 1 to 10 and the way to set up a chess board. Beneath the chess board mural can be a large scale chess board for the children to play with 1 to 2 feet tall chess pieces made out of cardboard or wood.

   On black top, concrete areas and sidewalks, maps of the U.S. or state can be drawn to scale. Patterns using vivid colors; concentric rings to help children form themselves into a circle can be created. A space station; a river with a crocodile; a hopscotch plan and a numbered snake are other examples. Some of these can also be used for teaching singing games or for drama and movement.

5. *Creative Play Areas* (Any Grade Level). Again books are written on this topic but here are a few suggestions for developing play areas that better match the needs and interests of children. It is well known that children, when provided the opportunities, will choose natural areas and simple facilities for creative play, rather than mechanical apparatus and gadgets. Thus, creative play areas should provide opportunities for swinging, balancing, climbing, dramatization, hanging, jumping, running, leaping, throwing, hopping, and constructing.

   Some suggestions which capitalize on natural features that may exist or be created are to develop or install:

   a. *Hills* for sledding down using cardboard boxes, saucers, for running up and down.

   b. *Ponds* for ice skating, fishing, wading and sailing toy boats.

c.   *Shrubs and Trees* for beautification and for climbing.

d.   *Boulders* for climbing and jumping.

e.   *Ravines* for climbing, constructing bridges, etc., jumping across.

f.   *Streams* for fishing, wading, sailing toy boats, constructing bridges and dams.

Natural play equipment that could be considered are:

a.   Telephone poles, tree stumps, railroad ties—mounted for balancing (high and low balance beams).

b.   Culverts—painted, unpainted, grouped to resemble animals and insects, made into a short tunnel under a hill—horizontal or vertical—holes cut in them for climbing.

c.   "Animals" made from logs—trimmed, painted, joined together.

d.   Varying lengths of logs—6 feet and less—stood vertically side by side for climbing and jumping.

e.   Tires planted in ground for leaping over, running obstacle course and laid flat for leaping, jumping and as sand boxes.

f.   Flat rocks, bricks forming squares, or concrete squares set into the ground forming various paths and patterns for leaping, skipping and jumping.

g.   Old fire engine and old row boats brightly painted and set in the ground.

h.   Rubber conical street markers.

i.   Obstacle course made of various combinations of the preceding.

C. *Soil*

1. *What can you Find?* (Primary). This activity should point out the importance of soil in plant growth.

    a. Go to the school site. Have students work in small groups and each group should toss a hula hoop to the ground with eyes closed. Each group should then examine the area within the hoop closely to see what they can find. They can list things in two categories: living and non-living. Did they include the soil?

    b. Now have them do it again on a sidewalk or in the parking lot. What do they predict they will find? Were they right? What makes each area different? (Perhaps discuss the fact that the reason there were fewer plants and animals on the sidewalk was because there was little or no soil to support plants, thus no food or shelter for animals on the sidewalk.)

2. *Earthworms and Soil* (Intermediate). The soil provides a home for many animals. The earthworm is one animal that lives there and also contributes much to the quality of the soil. This can be discovered by having students make earthworm homes.

    a. Students will need a jar. Fill the bottom with dark soil, called humus. Fill the top with sand. Cover with dead leaves. Add earthworms, cover the jar with dark paper.

    b. Things to investigate: Watch the soil. What happens? Keep a record. Watch the worm as it moves. Use a magnifying glass. How does it move?

    c. What do earthworms eat? How can you tell they are eating? (Droppings called "Castings"—digested organic material. The digestion of food from soil helps cultivate the soil because the earthworm has a gizzard which grinds up what the worm ingests. The castings actually enrich the soils for the plants. The burrows of the earthworm also aerate soil.)

    d. How are earthworms adapted to their environment? Pretend you are an earthworm. Write about your life.

    e. Why are earthworms important? Draw a picture that shows how earthworms help the environment.

D. *Minibeasts*

1. *Ant Watching* (Intermediate and Upper). Ants can be found just about everywhere on land. Several suggestions for investigating ants are provided here. Take the children to a place where you know ants can be found, perhaps where there is a nest or where there are ant runs. Each pair of children should have a magnifying glass and pencil. A handout with some of the following questions can be provided to give guidance or you can just say "write down all you can find out about ants."

    a. How many different kinds of ants do you see?

    b. How are they different? Size, shape, color, or other.

    c. Look at one ant closely with a magnifying glass.
        How many legs does it have?
        Does it have antennae or feelers?
        Does it have wings?
        Does it have eyes?
        How many body parts does it have?
        Draw a picture of an ant.
        From which part of the body do the legs come from?

    d. Watch an ant that is carrying something.

        What is it carrying?
        How big is its load?
        Does the ant keep moving steadily or stop and go?
        Does it move in the same direction all the time?
        What happens when it meets another ant?
        Does it act the same with all the ants it meets?
        Put something in the way of an ant that is carrying a load. What does it do?

    e. Determine the direction an ant appears to be going. With a moistened finger, draw a line on the sidewalk across the path. What happens?

    f. Look at an ant hill. What is it made from? Draw a picture of the ant hill.

    g. Put a piece of food a short distance from an ant hill.

        Use a watch to time how long it takes before the first ant finds it. What does it do when it finds it? Do other ants come? What happens when more than one ant finds the food?

    h. Put a small piece of meat, a small piece of bread, a little sugar and a little lettuce on the ground. Watch until an ant comes. Which kind of food does it go to most?

2. *Spiders*. Similar kinds of observations and activities can be done with spiders including these additions.

    a. Describe and sketch spider webs. How does the web feel?

    b. Where does the spider live (on a building, in the ground, etc.).

    c. What has the spider eaten?

    d. Can you entice the spider out of its nest or hole? (Because some spiders are harmful, it is not safe to put your hand in a spiders nest or hole). Use a stick after you have observed the nest—if you want to prod the spider out.

    e. If you see the spider, how big is it? What color is it? How many body parts? How many legs? How long are the legs? How fast does it travel?

E. *School Cracks:* You must be cracked! Use cracks in teaching. (Any Grade Level)

1. Look around the school site for cracks in the sidewalk, asphalt, buildings. Look for cracks in dried soil, trunks of trees, anywhere. Have children investigate these cracks. Are there patterns as to where cracks are found? Are there patterns within the cracks?

2. Have children take a closer look at cracks and inside cracks with magnifying glasses. What can be seen? If you find any plants or animals in the cracks, can you find the same life anywhere else?

3. What do you think caused the cracks? Do you think the cracks change during the school year? If so, keep a record of the size, shape, direction, length, etc., over a period of time.

4. Are there any geometric patterns made by cracks? Use tracing paper or thin paper and crayon to make tracings (rubbings) of various cracks. Create colorful designs with the rubbings.

5. Do cracks have any economic effect on people? If so, what? Determine the environment of cracks with regard to temperature, light intensity and moisture.

6. Study the sequence of soil development as related to cracks in rocks and pavement.

School Cracks such as these can be traced (rubbing technique) for later study back in the classroom.

IV. **Persistent Problems**

A. *Noise Pollution* (Any Grade Level). As a lead up, some of the activities dealing with observations of sounds listed previously can be used to introduce that some sounds can be harmful or annoying. These can be followed by activities investigating noise as a pollution. Here is one of each kind of activity.

1. *Sounds Around You.* (Primary and Intermediate)

   a. Sounds are all around you. They are part of your environment. Take students on a sound hike to different places in the school and on the school site. Listen for 60 seconds. Have students think of one sound they heard and draw a picture showing what made that sound.

   b. A follow up discussion can be had about the following: What sounds help people? Have students make a collage of the pictures they drew that show sounds that help people.

   c. Were any sounds natural sounds? Make a collage of natural sounds. Were any sounds man-made? Follow up activities could involve students taking tape recorders to different locations in the environment. Bring the recording back to class and have classmates guess where they were recorded.

2. *What is Noise?* (Intermediate) Discuss students ideas about noise. What is it? Do they like it? Is it good for you?

   a. Have students conduct a survey of their school or home and record all the noise producers. How do they affect people? What can be done about noise? How can we help?

   b. Some additional thoughts and activities. Have students draw a cartoon that shows how noise might bother someone.

   c. Some noises can cause hearing damage. Some people hear a lot of noise in their jobs. Make a list of these jobs. How are people protected from noise? Try to find out.

   d. Be a noise-detective. Use a tape recorder. Record the noises in your classroom and on the school site. Identify the noise producers. Can you lower the noise in your classroom and school site? Try it.

B. *Litter or Solid Waste*

1. *Solid Waste in Our Schools* (Upper)

a. Have your students collect the waste from several classroons over a period of several days. For a representative sample you may want to collect material from several types of classes, i.e., art, shop, home economics, the teacher's lounge, English, etc. Once the material is collected, have the students separate the trash into groupings of similar material.

b. Let the students create their own separation system. At this point a discussion on renewable and non-renewable resources, biodegradable and non-biodegradable materials, and inorganic or organic substances can be conducted.

c. Once the materials have been sorted, charts can be prepared listing composition, original source or sources, and destination of the trash collected.

d. This process should create considerable discussion on such topics as:

What is waste?
Where will all the waste go? Why?
What effect will this have on the environment?
Are there alternative solutions to waste disposal?
How could you cut down on the waste at your school?
How could you cut down on the waste at your home?

e. As a follow up to this activity, have the class trace some of the throw aways through their complete manufacturing and distribution process. Discuss what all is involved in the process.

f. Visit the local waste disposal plant or have a representative of the local sanitation department come in and talk to the class about the local situation.

g. Investigate the possibility of setting up a recycling station on or near your school.

2. *Litter, Litter, Everywhere* (Intermediate)

a. Have the class work in teams of three. Each team should be assigned to a different location in and around the school. Have them complete the following data sheet:

Observations of Litter in Our Environment

Describe the Litter	Where Did You See It?	How Was the Litter Harming the Environment?	What Did You Do about It?

b. Follow up discussions:
Litter is trash left on the ground. What is wrong with litter? What does it do?

c. Make a litter bag. Color it. Take a walk around the school. Pick up the litter and place in the bag.

d. Utilize the idea above to find out what types of litter are found. Who puts the litter there? Could any of the litter have been used again? Find a way to reuse some of the litter. Where was lots of litter found? Try to have a litter barrel placed there.

3. *Litter Survey* (Similar to previous but for Upper grades). Organize the class into groups of three and have each group assigned to a different area of the school or school grounds. Have them collect the following information: places where they see litter, kind of litter it is, amount of litter. Have each group draw a map of their area, use symbols for the types of litter they found, i.e., paper, plastic, glass, cans, other. Collect all the litter they find.

Follow up activities and discussion:

a. Did they find a place where no litter was found? Why is there no litter there?

b. Start an anti-litter campaign. Discuss how the class can educate their friends at school without causing more litter or solid waste? Examples: try creating a spot announcement about preventing litter. See if you can give it to other classes.

c. Make a survey of your community. Are there places where litter collects? See what you can do about it.

d. Measure the volume of the litter you found. If this much builds up in one day, how much will there be in a week? Month? Year? (Hint: Volume = Length × Width × Height).

e. Use some of the litter you found to make a garbage collage.

4. *Don't Throw It Away—Recycle It* (Intermediate). Recycle means "to use over." Have class list some of the things they throw away. How many of these could be reused? Have each student select one of the things they think they could reuse and hold a recycling fair to display the ways things can be reused. Who found the most ways for any one item?

Related discussions and activities:

a. Why is recycling important? (Most things are made from natural resources—some are renewable, i.e., new trees can be grown, and some are non-renewable, i.e., aluminum cannot be replaced: Recycling conserves our natural resources, makes less garbage and saves money).

b. What does a recycling plant do? Find out. Bottles and cans go in the garbage. Where do they go? What happens to them?

c. Collect some reusable items such as glass jars and aluminum cans. Either sell them and use the money to help the environment or make a present out of these items. If you make a present add a message that lists five ways to recycle things. Give it to someone you like.

5. *Recycling a Soil Compost* (Intermediate and Upper). Leaves are forever falling. Grass is always growing. Do they reach the sky? Why not? These things do die like other living things. They fall to the ground, decay or decompose and become part of the soil. Have the class make a compost pile to investigate how nature decomposes organic matter into particles that can be part of the soil. Are there some things that do not decompose as well as others?

a. Gather a collection of garbage, grass clippings and litter. Dig a hole approximately 2′ × 6′ and 3′ deep. Begin the activity by recording everything that goes in the pile and have students record predictions of what will happen to each type of debris. Record also the temperature of the compost pile on the first day. To place debris in hole alternate layers of garbage and dirt. (Note: the compost will not smell if meat is excluded). For a shorter method, begin by blending or cutting up the garbage parts before adding. Also, turn the compost every day or two.

b. Have students insert a thermometer each day to record the temperature. The temperature should rise as the decay action proceeds. The breaking down of natural materials produces heat. When the action of the decomposers is finished, the temperature will return to normal.

c. After four days have the students dig up some of the pile. Are there any changes? Record these observations. Wait two weeks and repeat.

d. Does man made litter disappear? What causes decay? Why is decay good? Use the compost. It makes an excellent fertilizer for plants growing in the classroom or at home.

e. Have each student examine their own garbage at home. What things will decay? What will not?

Final Note on Persistent Problems

In most of the previous activities on persistent problems, suggestions were provided for children to become "active" problem solvers. Too often we involve children in investigations that lead to understandings but fall short of having them participate in the citizenship role of doing something to resolve recognized problems. In addition to identifying a problem, collecting and recording data in an attempt to find out more about the problem, children should be allowed to conduct the following important steps in active problem solving:

1. Identify alternative solutions and the implications of each. What trade off will have to be made? What values and issues will emerge?

2. Take some action or actions on the basis of the solutions selected.

3. Assess the results of the action.

This latter step may start the whole cycle of problem solving all over again if a new problem has been created.

Chapter 7
Activities for the Urban Environment

Introduction

Three fourths of the nation's children live in cities. Beyond the grounds of the urban school, rich outdoor resources for experiencing various concepts, processes, phenomenon, and problems can be found. All that is required is a little thought and imagination on the part of the teacher to think of or find learning laboratories among the glass, steel, and concrete of the city.

With transportation costs rising, it is essential that alternative, less expensive, and less time consuming outdoor experiences be found. Besides, a trip once or twice a year to a "natural area" will not suffice, valuable though the experiences may be, in helping urban children develop ecological consciousnesses. Furthermore, if outdoor education is to be relevant to the urban child, much of it must occur within the settings where children live.

This chapter provides activity suggestions within the four theme categories of concepts, processes, natural and man-made phenomenon, and persistent problems. First, the following flow diagram may help you think of additional suggestions for activities.

Urban Environmental Flow Chart

I. Concepts

A. *Change*—Both natural and man-made changes occur constantly in an urban environment. Children can learn to recognize many changes, attempt to determine causes, and assess whether the changes are beneficial or harmful to the urban environment.

   1. *Natural Weathering* (Intermediate and Upper). Weathering caused by rain, snow, heat and cold slowly deteriorates the materials of most buildings.

   Take children to a location in the city where buildings have been exposed to any of the weathering factors identified above. Look for evidence of weathering, i.e., broken bricks, chipped walls, worn stone, chipped paint or worn wood. Find places on the same building where there is no weathering. What are the differences?

   Are there similarities from building to building that all have the same exposure to the sun, rain, etc.

   Find out the age of the buildings you are investigating. How long has it taken to create the amount of weathering you've observed. Predict the condition of the building in ten more years.

   2. *Man-made Weathering* (Intermediate and Upper). Some of the weathering observed in buildings may actually have been caused by man. Have students look for places on walls, buildings, in alleys, on streets, where man may have caused weathering damage. These are exhibited in places where loading carts and automobiles have struck buildings, and damaged bricks, i.e., corners of buildings, sidewalks, or in alleys.

   Which is more destructive—natural or man-made weathering?

   3. *Construction Sites* (Intermediate and Upper). Are there areas near school that are changing rapidly—tearing down of old buildings, new construction, new parks, new stores and parking lots? Changes can be noted over a period of weeks or months.

   If a new home is being constructed, the following can be studied:

   a. In what order are the jobs involved in building being done?
   b. Could the sizes of different parts of a house be estimated or measured?
   c. What materials are being used?
   d. What does one workman do with the materials at his disposal?
   e. If it is possible to get permission, collections could be made of the materials used in building the house.

   Often such man-made changes will cause observable changes in the plant and animal life as well as in temperature and humidity. Have children check it out.

   Do the changes alter the kinds and/or numbers of dwelling places and sources of food for animals? What evidence of the presence of plants and animals are there before, during, and after the changes in the building site?

   4. *Interviews About Change* (Intermediate and Upper). Children can interview older people in the community to learn about changes in the local environment during their lifetimes. Include such things as changes in the number of people; land use changes; new industries, and their impact; changes in weather and changes in transportation systems. What effect has each of these changes had on soil, water, animals, and people?

B. *Habitat*

1. *Habitat Survey* (Intermediate and Upper). Take the children on a walk in the neighborhood or city to find habitats or places where plants or animals live. Look for places where birds, mammals, insects, and plants can be found.

2. *Building Habitats* (Intermediate and Upper). Many dwelling places used by small animals are a result of man's activity. For example, the design of older buildings offers nesting and roosting places for house sparrows, pigeons, and starlings.

Are there changes in the sizes of these herd populations as new buildings replace the old?

Determine ways of increasing or decreasing the urban habitats.

C. *Adaptation* (Intermediate and Upper). Generally speaking, an animal lives where it does because it is able to adapt to and survive where it is. This means it is able to find food and shelter and that it's reproductive rate is at least as great as it's death rate. House sparrows, pigeons, starlings, and squirrels are probably the most common city animals.

Take children for a walk to find out where these animals live. Find out what these animals eat by watching them.

D. *I Spy: Shapes and Angles* (Primary and Intermediate). Buildings are combinations of rectangles, squares, triangles, and sometimes circles. You can take children for an "I Spy" walk to look for these various shapes. When you get to a certain location you or a child can say for example, "I spy a triangle" and then students must guess where the triangle is you've spied. Children could follow up by drawing the objects with the shapes they've spied.

For middle grade children, the search for different kinds of angles can be handled the same way. If children look carefully they can find corners making different kinds of angles where two lines meet. What sorts of angles can be found most easily? Look for these angles:

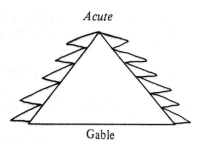

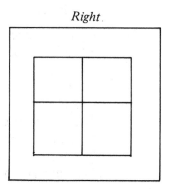

The City Hall building of Tempe, Arizona, offers many geometric shapes to observe and investigate.

II. **Processes**

A. *Observation*

1. *Searching for Animal Signs* (Intermediate). The following can be used as a guide sheet for children to follow independently or in small groups:

a. You often know animals have been around even though you don't see them. Remember that man is an animal. Here are some ways you can tell that he has been around.

Go to the neighborhood or city and close your eyes. Listen to all the sounds you hear that are made by man. Which of the following are found:

____ footsteps	____ singing	____ motorcycles
____ airplanes	____ garbage trucks	____ hammering
____ cars	____ car horns	____ trains
____ music	____ sirens	____ cans clanging
____ talking	____ trucks	____ others
____ laughing	____ whistles	

b. Animals sometimes leave signs they have been around. Think of signs that indicate that people have been in the neighborhood or city. Test the signs you can find.

c. Other creatures besides man live in the city. They create signs you can also hear, see and smell.
What animals can you see in the city? What animals can you hear in the city? What other signs of animals can you find?

d. Which of the following animal signs can you find in the city? (This can be done as a scavenger hunt).

____ feathers

____ nut shells or pine cones that have been chewed

____ webs

____ cocoons

____ droppings

____ worm castings (droppings)

____ mounds of dirt

____ bird nests

____ holes in leaves

____ footprints

B. *Measurement*

    1. *City Water Ways* (Intermediate and Upper). Locate a street near the school. Determine if the street is level from one side to the other by stretching a cord across the street; allow each end to rest on the curb; pull the string taut. Using a ruler or meter stick, measure the distance from the string to the surface near the middle of the street, 1/4 of the way across, 3/4 of the way across, and near the curb.

        Diagram your findings. If the measurements are the same in the middle of the street as at the curbs, the street surface is on a single plane.

        To measure whether the street is level longitudinally, use a small carpenters string level and measure 50 feet down the street.

        Discuss and do the following:

        a. How can the shape or level of the street best be described? Can you make a cross-sectional sketch?

        b. Does this shape assist in the run off of rainwater from the street? Why? How?

        c. What waste of water resources is represented by "storm water" runoff or over watering of lawns that run into the street?

        d. How could the waste be reduced? How could the waste water be utilized?

III. Phenomenon

A. *Garbage Cans* (Intermediate and Upper). The study of garbage cans and the garbage in them can lead to investigations in the other three categories of themes. For instance, cans can be used to exemplify varying degrees of change related to natural and man caused weathering and damage. Also cans can be used for classifying exercises related to age. In deciding age, students can look for signs such as dents, rust or discoloration. Further classification can relate to size and material from which the cans are made. With permission from owners and ample health care the contents of some garbage cans can be classified as to whether the material is biodegradeable or nonbiodegradeable. Kinds of material (plastic, metal, wood and glass) can also be categorized. Anthropological questions or problems can also be investigated. Such questions as: "What kind of store or business does the can belong to—based on the contents?" "What can you tell about the lifestyles of the people who use the can?" can be investigated.

Finally, a whole study of who picks up the garbage and where is it taken can be conducted. As a follow up, students can visit recycling plants, garbage dumps and land fills to find out what happens to the garbage in their cities.

B. *City Water* (Upper Grades). Many of us take our supply of water for granted. We're pretty confident that when we turn on the faucet, water will come out. But where does it come from? How much does it cost? Will the supply last forever?

Call, visit, or read about your local water treatment plant. Here are some questions to inquire about:

1. Where does my water come from?
2. How is the water treated before it reaches me?
3. How does the water reach my home?
4. Is there enough water for all the people and industries in the area?
5. How much does the water cost?
6. Will there be enough water if the population grows at the same rate? At a greater rate?
7. What are some special problems about water in this area?
8. Is there enough water to continue present agricultural practices?

Use your information in a class discussion on local water resources. Make a chart showing the flow of water in your area from its source to your home.

Using the chart as an outline, do a large mural showing the flow of water to your home.

An extension of this should be: Where does the water go from there? Where does it go after I have used it? What happens to the water I use in my swimming pool? The water that I use to water the lawn? Wash my car?

Follow this step by step. Do a flow chart from your home to the sea. Show where, at certain steps, some of the water is recycled into the system (evaporation from pools, irrigation, sewage ponds, etc.). Extend the first mural you did to include your use and where the water goes from there.

Is water ever "lost"? Is water a renewable resource? How far does water travel to you? From you to the sea? From the sea back to you? How long may parts of this cycle take?

C. *Vacant Lot* (Intermediate and Upper). Are vacant lots really vacant? Locate a vacant lot and get permission from the owner to conduct a study there. Divide the class into groups of 3 to 5 students and have each group stake out a plot of 12 feet (4 meters) square. Each team should do the following in their plot:

1. Look for signs of animal life such as holes, tracks, earth mounds or ant hills, animal droppings and spider webs.
2. Inventory the kinds and varieties of plant life.
3. Draw a map of their plot which indicates locations of plants and animals (or their signs). Later, maps could be combined to create a map of the vacant lot.

Map making is greatly enhanced when children are able to use the compass to assist them.

4. Find evidence of use by some animals that don't live there.
5. Find evidence of some animals preying on others.
6. Prove that certain plants grow better in certain locations.

As follow up, each group can prepare a presentation to illustrate the value of vacant lots in providing plant and animal habitats.

D. *Plants in the Neighborhood* (Any Grade). While some school sites may have few trees, shrubs and flowers to observe and investigate, there are usually areas within a city (such as a park, boulevard, or a resident's yard) where large varieties of plants can be found. Seek out city locations where plants can be studied and take students there to conduct a wide variety of plant activities.

Some possible starter suggestions would be to investigate:

1. Whether the plants were put there by people or not.
2. What's the difference between a tree and a shrub?

3. Which plants were not put there by people?
4. Can you find plants in cracks on sidewalks, around telephone poles, around street trees, in vacant lots, etc.

Additional activities could be to invite a representative of the parks department or city who can answer questions about the plants in the city planted by the city. Such things may be asked:

1. When were certain plants planted?
2. Why were certain plants chosen?
3. What do you do to care for them?
4. What plans for the future are there for the cities plants?

IV. **Persistent Problems**

A. *Conducting Surveys.* (Intermediate and Upper). Many problems of the urban environment can be identified or investigated by the development and administration of surveys and questionnaires. Samples of the kinds of information that can be collected are as follows:

1. How long have people lived where they are?
2. How old are the buildings?
3. How many people live in houses or apartments?
4. Where do people buy their food?
5. Where do they buy their clothes?
6. How far and with what means do people drive to work?
7. About businesses:

    a. How long have they been there?
    b. Are they parts of bigger companies?
    c. Do they sell things?
    d. Do they make things?
    e. Do they do things for people?
    f. How many people work there?

8. Impact of local shopping center and community.
9. Determining what is in a city block.
10. Inventory and classification of historic strucures within the central business district.

B. *Do Fast Food and Take Out Industries Waste Paper?* (Upper Grades). The take-out, fast-food industry has a big appetite for paper. It uses hamburger wrappers; boxes for the wrapped hamburgers; cardboard trays for the bag and the box and the wrappers; napkins; straws wrapped in paper; salt, pepper, sugar and powdered cream in paper packets; coffee cups; soft drink cups. And all the packaging is discarded within 15 minutes after its contents are consumed, a practice that contributes to the country's solid waste problem. Energy studies show that the equivalent of 12.7 million tons of coal and a sustained yield of 315 square miles of forest was used to provide packaging materials for hamburgers sold by just one fast-food chain in 1971 (Chicago Sun Times, Monday, October 30, 1972, "Fast Foods Squandering U.S. Resources" by Bruce Ingersoll).

This activity examines the trade-offs, economic and environmental, involved in the consumption of resources through packaging.

Divide the class into small groups. Each group should survey a local fast-food resturant to find out how much paper it uses in a given period of time, such as a week or a month. Before beginning the survey, students should make up a questionnaire to be used when they interview the restaurant manager.

Suggested questions are:

1. What items made of paper does your establishment use?
2. How many of each item do you use per (insert time period)?
3. What companies supply these paper items?
4. Why do you use paper packaging? (Answers might relate to cost, convenience, health codes, etc.)
5. Do you think you are overpackaging your products? (Remember, you want to keep the restaurant manager friendly, so be careful how students phrase this question.)

6. What percentage of the total cost of your product does the packaging represent?
7. How much do your employees make per hour?
8. Where and how do you dispose of your restaurant's solid waste (e.g., landfill, incinerate, recycle, etc.)?

When students have completed their interviews and tabulated their data, explore some of the following questions:

1. What were the principal reasons given for the use of paper packaging?
2. Are any of the items used by the fast-food outlets produced locally? If so, how many jobs are dependent upon sales of these products? (Don't forget printing, transportation, manufacturing of machines to print, making paper, etc.)

C. *Cemetery Search* (Intermediate and Upper). Is the urban environment becoming overcrowded? One of the reasons for this may be due to the fact that people are just living longer than they did in the past. One way to find out if people are living longer is to take a trip to a cemetery. Once there, children can divide up the area and collect information to complete the following chart:

Death Rates

Age at Death	Before 1900	1900-1925	1926-1950	1951-1975	1976-2000
0-5					
6-10					
11-20					
21-30					
31-40					
41-50					
etc.					

Age at death can be calculated by the children and placed in the chart. Discussion can relate to what is happening to the population of the United States based on the data collected.

D. *Community Beautification* (Intermediate and Upper). Quite often unattractive sites in a community are overlooked by the people living there. In an attempt to sensitize students to overlooked distractions the students can pretend they are first time visitors to the community. Take them on a walk and have them pretend they are seeing things for the first time.

As visitors, are there problems or blemishes that detract from the beauty that can be corrected? To guide their observations and suggestions have students discuss and complete the following chart:

Visitors View of the Community

Problems	Location	Slight Problem	Serious Problem
1. Litter and junk on road right-of-way			
2. Dead trees, shrubs, plants			
3. Billboards, abandoned or in need of attention			
4. Unsightly views: dumps, gravel pits, other			
5. Junk or debris along rivers, streams, lakes			
6. Abandoned autos			
7. Visible erosion on any part of highway			
8. Mailboxes in poor condition			
9. Condition of lawns, neatness, landscaping			
10. Unsightly advertisements and signs			
11. Other			

E.   *Transportation* (Intermediate and Upper). How does the need for transportation effect the environment?

As a class, list all the possible methods of transportation in your area. Then make a map of the area around your school showing:

1. Bike Paths
2. Roadways
3. Mass transit (buses, trains)
4. Expressways
5. Sidewalks
6. Parking lots
7. (Add any others in your area)

Now list in order from largest to smallest which of the above takes up the most land.

Using a data card such as the following, compile a list of the ways each method of transportation listed effects the environment. For example, does walking have any effect on air pollution? Water pollution? Does driving a car have any effect on air pollution?

Data Card on Transportation

Type of Transportation	Way It Affects the Environment					Is It Available in Your Community?
	Air	Water	Land	Noise	Liter	
Walking						
Bicycle						
Automobile						
Bus						
Plane						
Train						
Monorail						

When you've completed the transportation data card, discuss the impact each type of transportation in your area has on the environment. Which ways help or do not hinder the environment and why? Which ways hinder the environment? How and Why?

What steps can you as a class take to make others aware of the problems? What can you as a class or as individuals do to lessen the negative effects of transportation pollution?

F. *Air Pollution.* Air pollution is caused by many sources—both natural (dust) and man-made (automobiles). The activities which follow provide suggestions for measuring air pollution. Follow up activities can lead to discovering actual sources and attempting to make others aware of this information. All of these are for intermediate and upper grades.

1. *Measuring Dust in the Air: Approach I*

    Procedure:

    a. Cover two cardboard squares with 6″ strips of flypaper, sticky side out.
    b. Put one square in a box where air currents cannot reach it. Place other squares outdoors.
    c. After three days, observe and compare both squares using the microscope.
    d. Keep a record of the weather for a month, and every three days compare the two squares.
    e. Is there a connection with the amount of dust in the air and the weather during the month? Explain and discuss.

2. *Measuring Air Pollution: Approach II*

    Materials: Bucket—2 clean white rags—plastic bag

    Procedure:

    a. Clean out the bucket very carefully and thoroughly first.
    b. Now wipe it again with your clean white cloth. It should stay clean.
    c. Place the cloth in a plastic bag and label it.
    d. Now place the bucket outside in a place where it will not get knocked over.
    e. Leave it there for thirty days.
    f. Now take your second clean white cloth and wipe out the bucket.

    Results:

    a. Undoubtedly, the second cloth will be dirtier.
    b. Observe what the dirt particles are.
    c. What does this do to your lungs?

    Variations:

    a. Try this with buckets of water. The water in both procedures can be checked by running through a filter (filter paper in a funnel).
    b. Which comes out cleaner?

3. *Measuring Air Pollution—Approach III*

    Materials: 2 metal buckets—water—heat source

    Procedure:

    a. Pour 6 to 8 inches of water in the metal bucket.
    b. Set the bucket outside for 30 days where it will not be disturbed.
    c. Take the second bucket with the same amount of clean water and boil dry.
    d. Do the same with the first bucket.
    e. Compare the residue of each.

    Results:

    a. The first bucket should show more particles.
    b. Estimate what this would be on your house . . . on your block.

    Follow up suggestions for discussions and more activities are as follows:

    a. Why is air important to living organisms?
    b. When can air be an enemy?

c.   How does air affect what you do?

d.   In what ways does the air affect the landscape?

e.   How has man negatively modified the air quality?

f.   How is he positively modifying the air quality?

g.   What are some of the esthetically appealing qualities of air?

h.   What does poor quality air do to your body?

i.   Could poor quality air permanently change the environment? If so, how?

j.   What are some of the recreational benefits of air?

G. *Community Areas* (Intermediate and Upper). This activity does not focus on pollution but on the purposes of the various areas within the community. The following types of areas should be discussed with the class:

1. *Pathways*—lines of movement (walks, bus routes, streets)
2. *Nodes*—small areas of intense focus where an observer may enter and feel a sense of belonging, safe, enclosed (small park, courtyard, intersection, intimate shopping center)
3. *Edges*—linear breaks in continuity (freeway, river, edge of hills)
4. *Landmarks*—identifiable objects or reference points (high-rise building, fountain)

Now take the class for a walk or ride in the community to identify those places that can be considered a pathway, node, edge, or landmark. What other categories can be created besides the four used here?

Once data is collected students can determine whether each item identified presents a problem or potential benefit to the community.

Reasons for studying the community using these four divisions are:

1. If a community has only one division, it is often a boring community.
2. If divisions are varied and strong, then a strong exciting community environment can exist.
3. If an area is dying out, nodes, points of interest, pathways, etc., might be created to strengthen the area in ways that contribute to the livability of the community.

As a follow-up to this activity and to a whole unit on the city, children working in groups—each group responsible for nodes, pathways, edges and landmarks, can create the ideal community. This can be a to-scale model using cardboard, clay, wood, styrofoam, etc., and cover the top of several tables in the classroom.

Chapter 8

Activities for the Water, Forest and Desert Environments

Introduction

The forest, water, and desert are three environments that have a natural attraction for most children. These can be experienced either on a one-day, overnight, or resident camping outing. Within each of the three phenomena themes, activities also relating to concepts, processes, and persistent problems can be generated. A few possibilities are suggested in this chapter. The following flow diagrams for each theme may suggest additional ideas.

I. **Water** (Lakes, Streams, and Rivers)

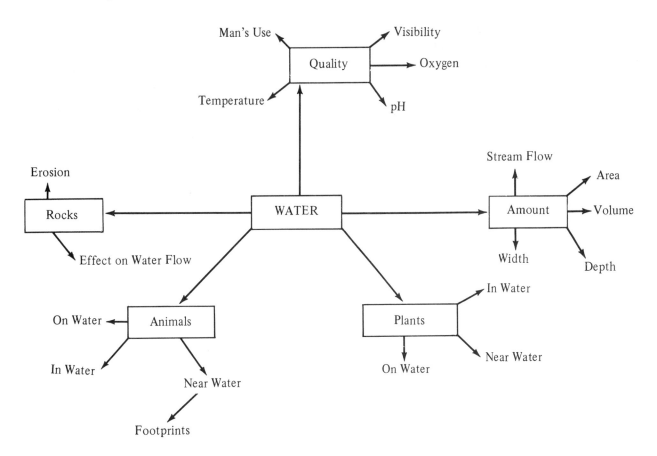

A. *Observing the Water Environment* (Any Grade Level). This is designed to be an introductory open discovery lesson, the purpose of which is to allow children to experience as much of the total environment as possible. Follow-up activities can allow children to investigate one aspect in depth.

As you approach the water (lake, river or stream) find a place where you can sit and look at the water. Ask the question "What do you observe?" Observations will probably relate to the plants, animals, air, rocks, the water.

Another key question to ask might be "What would you like to find out about the water environment?" This could lead to a variety of questions on problems the students could investigate—provided you have the right equipment to assist the children. Lessons which follow relate to many of the types of questions you can expect children to ask:

What lives there?
Where does the water come from?
Where does it go?
How did the lake, river, stream get its name?
What kind of plants can be found here?
How much water is there here?
Where would you expect to find animals in the water?
Is the water good to swim in or drink?
How cold is the water?
How deep is the water?

B. *What Lives in the Water?* (Any Grade Level). Provide children with dip nets, hand lens, plastic containers, and have them collect as many types of aquatic animals as possible. These can be placed in light colored plastic containers or white dish pans so that large numbers of children can observe the animals that are caught.

Armed with nets and containers, children soon discover ways of collecting water organisms from the middle of the stream.

Questions which can be investigated during this process: Where do you observe or find most of the animals? What are some guidelines that we need to consider in collecting aquatic life so our investigation will cause the least impact on the environment? What are some factors that affect the lives of animals in water? What do the animals eat? Which are predators and which are prey? How many different kinds of animals were found or observed?

As follow up, drawings of or collected examples of some of the animals can be identified using field guides. What similarities are there among the water animals? What differences are there? What classification system could be used to categorize the types of water animals found?

C. *Aquatic Animal Movement* (Primary, Intermediate). As another follow up of the previous activity, each student can select one of the aquatic animals they've observed and identified, then act out the movements of that animal. Other children try to guess what animal is being portrayed.

D. *Water Quality* (Upper Grades). There are many simple to use kits available for upper grade children to use to measure the oxygen content and pH of water. In addition, it is also quite simple to measure water temperature. Such activities can be carried out to find out how the water quality factors relate to the presence or absence of certain plant and animal life forms. The following charts can be used to aid students in making water quality predictions or as data to support observations of what plant and animal life was actually found.

Analyzing Data

pH RANGES THAT SUPPORT AQUATIC LIFE

MOST					NEUTRAL						MOST ALKALINE		
1	2	3	4	5	6	7	8	9	10	11	12	13	14

Bacteria 1.0 _____ 13.0

Plants
(algae, rooted, etc.)   6.5 _____ 12.0

Carp, suckers, catfish,
some insects   6.0 _____ 9.0

Bass, crappie   6.5 _____ 8.5

Snails, clams, mussels   7.0 _____ 9.0

Largest variety of
animals (trout, mayfly,
stonefly, caddis fly)   6.5 ____ 7.5

DISSOLVED OXYGEN REQUIREMENTS FOR NATIVE FISH AND OTHER AQUATIC LIFE

D.O. in parts per million

Cold-water Organisms including (salmon and trout) (below 68°)
  Spawning . . . . 7 ppm and above
  Growth and well-being. . . . . 6 ppm and above
Warm-water Organisms (including game fish such as bass, crappie) (above 68°)
  Growth and well-being. . . . . 5 ppm and above

TEMPERATURE RANGES (APPROXIMATE) REQUIRED FOR GROWTH OF CERTAIN ORGANISMS:

Temperature		Examples of Life
Greater than 68 (warm water)		Much plant life, many fish diseases. Most bass, crappie, bluegill, carp, catfish, caddis fly.
Less than 68 (cold water)	Upper range (55-68)	Some plant life, some fish diseases. Salmon, trout, Stonefly, mayfly, caddis fly, water beetles, striders
	Lower range (Less than 55)	Trout, caddis fly, stonefly, mayfly

Checking the water quality helps build group cooperation and problem solving
skills.

From the charts: What sorts of plants and animals would you expect to find? Were these found? Why or why not? Under what quality conditions would you expect to get different results than you did today?

Is the water safe to play in or drink? What else do we need to know before we answer that question?

A chart like the following can be used to collect water quality data to take back to the classroom for discussion.

Location of Water Sample (edge or middle of stream)	Time Taken	Temperature Water Air				pH		Useable Oxygen (ppm)	
		My Pred.	Act. Test	My Pred.	Act. Test	My Pre.	Act. Test	My Pred.	Act. Test

E. *Measuring Stream Flow* (Upper). The average person requires 200 gallons of water a day for drinking, cooking, washing, etc. How many people could this stream, river or lake (if there is an outlet in the lake leading to a stream or river) support? What measurements are needed in order to determine the amount of water in the stream? What is your prediction of the amount of water there is?

The following method of estimating the volume of water in a stream or river requires little equipment: yard or meter stick, a small wooden block or cork, wooden stakes, and a watch with a second hand.

1. Select an area of a stream without bends and with a nearly symmetrical bottom.
2. Measure the width of the stream in feet or meters. (W)
3. Measure the depth (D) in the center, in feet or meters.
4. Determine the surface velocity (V) by placing the small block of wood in the middle and recording the time required for it to float 10 feet or meters down stream. The average time of several trials will give more accuracy.
5. Compute the volume of stream flow in cubic feet/meters per second (F) using this formula:

$$F = W \times D \times V \times A$$

A is the bottom-factor constant; 0.8 if the stream bottom is rough (gravel or cobbles), 0.9 if the bottom is smooth (mud, sand, hardpan, or rock.)

A far more accurate method to find F is to divide the stream into three equally wide sections, using two wooden stakes to mark the divisions, and then find the flow of each section and add these together for the total flow.

Discussion Questions

1. Why is the second method more accurate?
2. Why is the constant A needed in the formula?
3. If a heavy local shower suddenly started, how would it effect stream flow?
4. Would precipitation in other parts of the surrounding mountains effect this stream?
5. What time of year will have the greatest flow? The least?
6. Would the shape of the stream bed effect the water velocity?
7. What possible accuracy errors exist here?
8. How many people could live off this amount of water?
9. If we were going to use some of this water for man's use, how much should be left to flow downsteam? Why?
10. How important is this stream, river or lake to a community? To the environment here?

Boats—built and ready for the Boat Race.

F. *Boat Races* (Any Grade Level). Children love to race boats in moving water. Provide children with a variety of materials to use as boats, sails, decorations, rudders, etc., and have them create a boat. Select a place in a stream or river that is somewhat unobstructed by limbs, plants or logs and have a race with the boats. This could lead to discussions both about boat construction (which was the fastest, slowest—ugliest, prettiest, etc.) and what characteristics about the stream or river helped or hindered the race. Where were the fastest and slowest places in the river? Was one side of the river faster than another?

This team provides encouragement for their boat during the Boat Race.

G. *Animal Tracks* (Intermediate and Upper). Lakes, streams and rivers are good places to find animal tracks. Children can be asked why. Children can also make predictions about the kinds of animal tracks that can be found. The tracks on mud or sand can present many interesting questions to persue such as:

1. What animal made them?
2. What direction was the animal moving?
3. How big was the animal?
4. Was the animal walking or running?
5. How fresh are the tracks?
6. Was the animal chasing something or running away from something?
7. Did the animal go into the water?
8. Is there any evidence the animal did more than drink from the water?
9. How many toes does the animal have?

H. *Making Plaster of Paris Casts of Animal Tracks* (Intermediate and Upper). Tracks can be easily copied using clay or plaster of paris. The casts can then be taken back to the classroom for follow up expression and investigation. Here's one recommended method of making casts:

1. Cut a strip of cardboard that can be folded into a ring that is about 3″ to 4″ high or cut a ring 3″ high out of a plastic jug. The ring should have a diameter big enough to fit over most animal tracks.
2. Mix plaster of paris. Judge the amount of water needed to fill the cardboard or plastic mold, then add plaster of paris to water, *not vise versa*. Add plaster of paris and stir until consistency of pancake batter.
3. Clear the area in and near the animal track of sticks, stones, leaves, etc.
4. Work the edges of the ring slightly into the ground with the edges of the ring about one inch away from the edge of the track.
5. Pour the plaster of paris into the mold and allow to sit for 30 minutes or so.
6. Carefully remove the cardboard or plastic ring and the cast. Take ring away from cast.

I. *Lake, River or Stream Mural* (Intermediate and Upper). As may have been discovered in the previous activities, plants and animals may be found distributed in distinct zones and bands around and across water areas.

Groups of children can investigate plant and animal life and environmental factors such as temperature, moisture in soil and pH within various zones including the middle of the water, near the edge of the water, the shore of the water, and one or two land zones that come near the water. Data collected by each group can then be translated into a large wall mural back in the classroom. The mural can then be studied and follow up activities and study can be enhanced by the information on the mural.

A forest ranger explains how the helicopter is used to help fight forest fires.

II. Forest

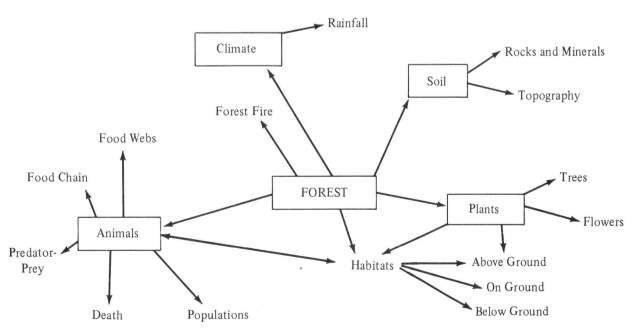

A. *Exploration Walk* (Primary and Intermediate). Even though teachers may not know names of specific plants or animals found in the forest (or any environment) they can lead a group of children on a nature walk and help children find out a great deal about the environment. The emphasis of this activity is on the processes of observing and comparing.

   Materials needed are a portable tape recorder and drawing materials.

   Directions

   1. From a starting point in the environment, determine a direction that cuts across the area (or follow an established path or trail).
   2. Begin walking in that direction and stop when you come to an interesting plant or tree.
   3. Turn on the tape recorder and ask the children to describe the properties of the plant or tree. Have the children tell about those things that seem to make it different from other trees. They may tell about the leaves (color, texture, shape, smell), thorns, height, bark (color, texture, smell), and the amount of shadow and shade.
   4. If you don't know the tree or plant's name, have the children make one up based on the main properties you've observed. Add this name to the tape recording. This is how many trees got their names anyway. Making up your own name also indicates to children that naming and classifying plants is a man-made process.
   5. Each time you come to a new tree or plant, perform the same task but also have the children tell into the tape recorder how each new tree is different and alike than the previous tree you observed.
   6. When you've observed and named about five or six different plants or trees, return to the starting point and listen to your tape recording.
   7. As the children listen to the tape, they can draw the plant or tree using their given properties. Each tree then can be labeled with the names they provided.
   8. During your walk you should not be limited to plants and trees. As an exploration type walk, other interesting things such as rocks, ant nests, insects and other animals might be observed and discussed in a similar way.

B. *Theme Walks* (Intermediate and Upper). In addition to the previous introductory inquiry walk, a variety of additional excursions into the forest can be conducted which focus on specific forest themes. Here are examples of some of these themes and questions that can be asked to encourage investigation:

   1. *Space*
       a.   How many different things are competing for this space?
       b.   What is the nature of the space? (Sunny, dry, high, low, wet, crowded)
       c.   Is there any relation to this space and the things we see here?
       d.   Which would only be here and probably not in other spaces? (i.e., cattails would only be found in a marsh)
       e.   Which might be found in other places?
       f.   What would seem to be the best use of this space?
       g.   Should man intervene to alter the space in any way?
       h.   What other uses might you suggest?
       i.   Has this space always been as we now see it?
       j.   What other living and non-living things might have been here in the past?

   2. *Food—What and how to use it.*
       a.   What sources of food are there?
       b.   What seems to be making use of this particular food?
       c.   Does there seem to be a need to increase the food supply?
       d.   Is there anything that man uses as food, i.e., apples, berries?

    e.   Do you see anything man might use as food in a crisis situation?

    f.   How might we increase the food for man and other animals?

    g.   Are there any particular problems in harvesting the food?

    h.   What natural materials are here for preparing food in emergencies?

3. *Travel Lanes and How to Use Them*

    a.   What is here that we will have to move out?

    b.   How are travel lanes connected to the food supply?

    c.   How has man hindered or helped travel lanes?

    d.   Does man have adequate travelling facilities in this area?

    e.   What might be done to improve the movement of animals in this area? (i.e., adequate cover).

    g.   What lane or path would you like to follow?

    h.   How do humans use natural trails intelligently? (i.e., map and compass trails, survival)

4. *Homes*

    a.   Do we see any signs of homes?

    b.   Where would we expect to find them?

    c.   What materials do we find that could be used to build homes?

    d.   What is here that man could use to provide a home or shelter?

    e.   Where would be a good and safe place to build a home?

5. *Habitat*

    a.   How would you describe the habitat?

    b.   What kinds of plants and animals probably live here?

    c.   How could and how will nature eventually change this habitat?

    d.   How will man most likely change this habitat?

    e.   What changes can you foresee as the area changes naturally?

6. *Cover*

    a.   Are there places for nesting cover?

    b.   Are there places of escape cover?

    c.   What types of cover seem to predominate?

    d.   In what ways does this contribute to a more interesting area?

7. *Water*

    a.   Where is there water for animals to be found besides a lake?

    b.   How is water used in this environment?

    c.   Is man doing anything to poison or pollute the environment?

    d.   Who or what else are using the water (birds, mammals, etc.)?

    e.   How deep is the water table?

    f.   What could cause a water shortage?

C. *Other Interesting Theme Walks* (Any Grade Level). Interesting themes to tie a field trip together are the following:

1. Animal homes	8. Travels to foreign lands	15. I am . . . blue, red, green
2. Plant homes	9. Travelers (Burdock)	
3. Community life	10. Air transportation	16. Nature's paint patch
4. Foreign born	11. Water transportation	17. Nature's tools
5. Natural citizens	12. Land transportation	18. Holes in the ground
6. Undesirable citizens	13. Stay at homes	19. Medicine chest
7. Weeds	14. Wingless air travelers	

D. *Stump Stalking* (Intermediate and Upper). Find a stump of a tree that has been cut down by man. Have children notice the tree rings inside the stump. These can tell many important things about the forest environment.

1. The number of annual rings can be counted to determine the trees age. Usually it takes five years for a tree to become large enough to grow a ring. Students will have to add this to the total number of rings counted.

2. Examine the width of the rings, from center to outer ring. Can you tell what the weather was like during certain years? When was it dry? When was it wet?

3. Look at the light colored spring wood. Why is it porous? Find the darker summer wood. Which of the two grew more rapidly? What was the shortest number of years that it took for the tree to grow two inches? What was the longest? Is there any sign of injury to the tree?

4. Examine the tree rings again and predict any major changes that may have occurred in the forest during the life of the tree.

5. Was the tree cut recently or a long time ago? How can you tell?

6. Is it possible to determine what tools were used to cut this tree?

7. Where did the man cutting the tree stand? Which way did the tree fall?

E. *Tree Bark* (Any Grade Level). An interesting way to study trees in any season is by investigating tree bark. Select two different types of trees for study.

1. *Bark Texture.* Use a piece of paper and a wax crayon to make a bark rubbing. Study the bark rubbing in each sample and describe and compare textures.

2. *Measuring Cracks.* How many cracks are there in a square of each bark sample? What is the distance across each crack? Do the cracks run vertically, horizontally or at an angle?

3. *Bark Color.* Color charts from a hardware store, lumber yard or paint store are useful in helping to detect difference in color shades between the two bark samples.

4. *Thickness of Bark.* An increment bore can be used to withdraw a core of the tree which will reveal the thickness of the bark. A simple hand drill with a small bit can also be used to drill a hole to determine bark thickness. Neither of these processes will harm the tree. When a drill is used, drilling can stop when white sawdust first comes out of the hole. A nail can then be inserted in the hole to measure the thickness of the bark.

F. *Plant Drama* (Any Grade Level). An excellent right brain activity involves the following creative dramatic activities.

Have students stand in the forest or indoors as though they were a large tree. Have them position arms, legs, body and attitude as though they were that tree. Then ask them to represent the actions and feelings of that tree if the following occurred:

1. During the development of a thunderstorm i.e., gentle breeze, light rain, heavier rain, thunder, lightening, light rain, gentle breeze, passing of the storm.
2. During a forest fire.
3. With a squirrel climbing the tree and building a nest in a branch.
4. With a person carving initials in the bark.
5. With a person cutting down the tree.

G. *From Seed to Tree* (Primary and Intermediate). Here's another dramatization that helps children develop an understanding and appreciation of how trees grow.

Pick a spot where everyone can spread out on the ground and sit down comfortably. Ask each child to think about a tree seed such as an acorn or seed from a pine cone. Because the first thing a seed must do in order to germinate is to be planted, the children should be encouraged to find a way to be planted. They can do this by poking a hole in the ground with their finger or stick and pretend they are planting themselves.

They can then lie flat down on the ground and think about growing. As they grow, they become taller so they should sit up slowly and eventually stand and reach out with their arms as far apart as possible.

As growing and grown trees, they must compete with each other for food, light, nutrients and space. Encourage children to symbolize this. Note that some trees die in the process.

H. *Forest Soil* (Intermediate and Upper). Select two or three locations within the forest where soil samples can be studied (i.e., under a tree stand, in a meadow, in an area not covered by trees). While specific investigations can be conducted on soil temperature, texture, structure, and pH, the following investigation leads to basic understandings about what soil is and what lives in soil that should be completed before the more analytical studies.

Teams of children investigating soil from underneath a forest tree.

1. *What is Soil and How Does it Differ in Each Sample?* Have students collect three different soil samples and lay these out on a table or card. Introduce the terms *litter* (identifiable dead things on surface), *duff* (partially decomposed organic matter—compacted), and *humas* (almost completely decomposed nonidentifiable organic matter). These are the layers of materials that can be found at the top of the soil. How do the three samples of soil differ with respect to these layers? What is found in each of these layers in each of these samples?

    Have the remaining soil layers from each sample to investigate differences in layers, color, texture, structure, temperature and pH. Other guides describe how to do this.

2. *What Lives in the Soil?* Use magnifying glasses to find out what organisms are found in the various three soil samples. Are there different and like things found in each sample? How do you think the organisms you found effect the soil?

III. **The Desert**

For children living in arid regions the desert is a rich resource for developing knowledges, appreciations, and skills related to various environmental relationships. The examples which follow are samples of experiences that sensitize children to both beauties and dangers of the desert. The following flow diagram, as in previous diagrams, should help stimulate additional ideas.

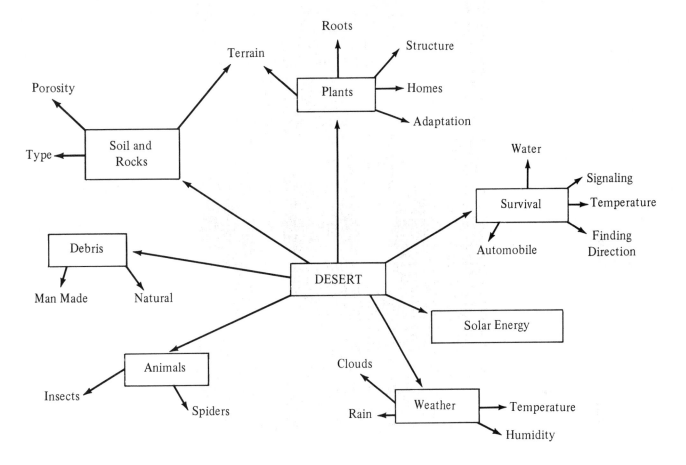

A. *Desert Survival.* Many people die every year in desert environments because of their lack of preparation and knowledge of the desert. With a little bit of knowledge and a lot of common sense, most people can enjoy and appreciate the desert safely. The following represent activities that not only help children develop inquiry skills, but can help provide knowledge of the desert and survival pointers that may save their lives some day.

1. *Finding Water* (Intermediate and Upper). Desert travelers should always carry water because the desert is a very unreliable source of water. Despite this fact, the search for water can provide an interesting inquiry (as long as the search is not an emergency survival situation). Start by identifying clues related to geography and plant and animal dependence on water as a means of determining where water might be found

   Here are some clues that may be discussed and investigated by children (as a learning—not survival activity).

   a. Watch for animal trails which may lead to water.
   b. Birds often circle over water holes. Quail travel to water in late afternoon and often roost in brush or trees near water. Doves fly to water (often many miles) in the morning and evening.
   c. Seeps and dips may be found in conjunction with rocky cliffs for some time after rains.
   d. Dry stream beds may have water near the surface. Dig at the lowest point on the outside of a bend in the stream channel. Dig until you hit wet sand. Water will (may) seep into the hole. Let the water settle and clear.
   e. Look for "indicator" plants which grow only where there is water: cotton-woods, sycamores, willows, hackberry, saltcedar, cattails, or arrowwood. Dig near these.
   f. The immature stalks of Agave, Yucca, Mescal, and Sotol contain moisture (they look like asparagus tips), or the main stalks may be split open and the pith chewed for moisture. The barrel cactus contains a high degree of moisture, but it is not possible to squeeze out the water, as the muscilaginous acid juice thickens rapidly.

   In addition to investigating such locations, discussions and demonstrations about how to purify water can be conducted. One other activity that may be conducted is the building of a *desert still.* Because construction instructions are given in most desert survival sources, it is not described here. It should be pointed out that as a survival technique, the still offers little hope of saving lives because of the body fluids and energy it takes to build. It is, however, a good activity to teach concepts related to moisture in air and how to retrieve it.

2. *Water Requirements for Survival* (Intermediate and Upper). Usually the best thing to do when lost in the desert is to stay in one place and seek shade. Students should be able to draw this conclusion by examining the following charts. This is a good activity to help children learn to read data tables. Once the charts have been analyzed, children can then make graphs to represent this data.

Water Requirement Charts[1]

A. Number of Days of Expected Survival in the Desert, No Walking at All:

Available Water per Man, U.S. Quarts	0	2	3	4	10	20
Max. Daily Shade Temp. F.	Days of Expected Survival					
120 degrees	2	2	2	2.5	3	4.5
110	3	3	3.5	4	5	7
100	5	5.5	6	7	9.5	13.5
90	7	8	9	10.5	15	23
80	9	10	11	13	19	29
70	10	11	12	14	20.5	32
60	10	11	12	14	21	32
50	10	11	12	14.5	21	32

B. Number of Days of Expected Survival in the Desert, Walking at Night until Exhausted and Resting Thereafter:

Available Water per Man, U.S. Quarts	0	1	2	4	10	20
Max. Daily Shade Temp. F.	Days of Expected Survival					
120 degrees	1	2	2	2.5	3	
110	2	2	2.5	3	3.5	
100	3	3.5	3.5	4.5	5.5	
90	5	5.5	5.5	6.5	8	
80	7	7.5	8	9.5	11.5	
70	7.5	8	9	10.5	13.5	
60	8	8.5	9	11	14	
50	8	8.5	9	11	14	

Note: The importance of temperature reduction to the survivor is highlighted by the preceding Chart A. Temperature−120°, water available−2 quarts, days of expected survival−2; reduce the temperature to 100° and 2 quarts of water will extend your life expectancy three times. This importance to a potential "survivor" cannot be overemphasized. Night travel, or better, no travel is stressed.

3. *Temperature and Survival* (Intermediate and Upper). From the previous chart it can also be discovered that temperature is an important variable in surviving in the desert. Once this has been determined, an activity can be conducted in the desert to determine those places in the desert where the "coolest" (by comparison) places can be found.

Armed with thermometers and measuring devices, the children can measure temperature at ground level—in the shade and in the open, six inches above the ground—in the shade and in the open, one foot above ground—in the shade and in the open and at different six inch or one foot intervals—in the shade and open.

The results can then be graphed. Where are the best places to be to survive the desert? What does this suggest about staying in one place versus trying to hike to safety during the day?

Additional variables to be measured could be the kind of surface on which the temperature is taken, i.e., on and above rock, gravel, dirt and wood.

(Note: It has been said that temperature differences between ground level and a few feet above the ground can be as high as 30°.)

4. *Signaling for Assistance* (Intermediate and Upper). There are several possible ways of sending signals over long distances to ask for assistance in a survival situation. Some of the ways include using fires and gun shots. While these are impractical to use in instructional situations with children, there are some signaling techniques which can provide inquiry experiences. These are:

   a. *Use of a Mirror to Signal.* A simple cosmetic mirror can be used effectively to attract attention from an aircraft or location where people might be found. A flash of reflected light can be seen for miles and is one of the easiest and most effective signals to use when the sun is out. Children will find the technique of using a mirror to signal an intriguing one. Here's one way to practice the skill:

Signaling with a mirror can be practiced just about anywhere.

   (1) Line the bottom of a box with aluminum foil. This represents the practice target.
   (2) Have students stand about ten feet away from the foil lined box.
   (3) They can take turns holding the mirror in one hand. To aim at the box they sight across the top of the mirror.
   (4) With the other hand held beyond the hand holding the mirror, form a "V" with your first two fingers and aim at the target through these fingers. Then drop the fingers.
   (5) When the box is hit correctly, the foil will flash back.
   (6) Practice with the box moved 20 feet away, then 30, 40 and 50 feet or more away.
   (7) Continue practice until a moving object can be hit.
   (8) It is not advisable to practice on airplanes or in the desert as this may be interpreted as a real survival situation.

Discussion Questions:

If lost in survival situation, what could be used as a mirror or reflecting device?

At what angle will one have to stand to the sun in order to get the sun light to reflect on a given target? This also can be practiced with the foil lined box. (What is the mathematics of angles of incidence and reflection?)

b.   *Use a Whistle.* While a sound does not carry as far as reflected light, the sound of a whistle does carry farther than the human voice. Two students, each with whistles can determine how far on the desert the whistle sound does carry. An interesting feature to investigate is: does a whistle sound carry farther with or without the little cork ball found in most whistles? Children can investigate this variable.

5. *The Automobile in Desert Survival* (Intermediate and Upper). Automobile breakdown in the desert is perhaps the largest cause of survival situations. People often have breakdowns in the desert without having planned ahead of time for such situations. They are without water and food, without maps, without the ability to move the car and without having told others where they might be found. Despite these facts, the same car, even totally disabled has many uses in helping save passengers lives. Children can be taken to a car and asked to brainstorm all the possible things that can be used on or in the car to help survive. Actual suggestions can even be tried out. Here are some of the possible uses of the car to help in survival situations:

a. First realize a disabled car with trunk and hood open is more visable from the air than people are. If you are overdue for your return, hopefully someone will notify authorities and planes, helicopters, four wheel drives and horsemen will be searching. If all these people are looking for a car rather than a man on foot, they will obviously have a much better chance of succeeding.

b. Seat covers, cushions and the seats can be taken from the car to the shade (and above ground level) to wait for rescuers.

c. Signal fires which can be seen from aircraft can be started by old maps or other articles found in the glove compartment. Also found in the glove compartment might be forgotten packs of matches. The car's cigarette lighter is another source of a fire starter.

d. Oil from the car can be used to make black smoke—visable during the day. Or, punch a hole in the gas tank to get gasoline to help ignite a big fire.

e. The lug wrench in the trunk can serve as a tool to do a number of jobs.

f. Rear view and side-mounted mirrors can be used as signalling devices.

g. If the car is completely disabled and cannot be used to get out, consider deflating the spare tire and burning it. Rubber makes black smoke and the fire should be visable for many miles.

h. Hub caps and floor mats are another source of shade. The mats may be used as makeshift shoes or as additional insulation from hot sand.

i. Generally, water from the radiator should not be used internally. However, the fluid can be used to moisten cloths to keep cool.

j. Oil or grease from the engine can be used to make streaks under the eyes (like football players) to keep sun glare off the face.

k. Hub caps can also be used to dig for and carry water.

l. Other—you brainstorm them.

B. *Plants*. Desert plants have many features that help them to adopt to extremes in temperature and low moisture. Many of the following activities deal with plant adaptations.

1. *Why are Cactus Fat?* (Intermediate and Upper). Wet two handkerchieves or paper towels of the same size. Crumple one into a round ball. Stretch the other out flat and straight. Pin both to a coat hanger.

   Have children predict what will happen if both are out in the sun. Observe. Which dries first? Which handkerchief is shaped like most cacti? What conclusions can you make about the fat shape of many cacti?

   What about the flat prickly-pear cactus? What does it do to conserve water? Do all cacti conserve water in this way too?

2. *Plant Life and Terrains.* (Intermediate and Upper). Divide the class into groups of three to five children. Each group should be assigned to a different terrain, i.e., flat ground, a wash, under a tree, near a desert road, and on different slopes (north, east, south, west) of a hill, butte or mountain.

   Within each area a segment of the land should be marked off, i.e., five square meters. Each group should then estimate the percentage of the land that is covered with vegetation. Names of the major plants found can be identified, if field guides are available.

   Next, each group should collect seeds from the marked off areas. How did each type of seed get there? How far might they have traveled? On return to the classroom, children can attempt to plant the seeds and see how long each takes to germinate.

   Each group can then display their data and share it with the other groups using charts, graphs and maps. Which type of terrain seemed to support the most plant life? Other activities may deal with why there were differences in the terrain.

3. *Saguaro Growth* (Intermediate and Upper). It is said a Saguaro, on the average, grows two inches a year. Estimate the age of several Saguaros found in the desert. Children can also discover whether it is true that the Saguaros are about 70 years old before they branch.

   Notice the holes in each cactus and guess probable causes. What does the cactus do when this happens? Can children find out what the secretion is?

   Examine the root system. How far below the surface are the roots? What approximate area do the roots cover? How can this be explained? What is the height/root ratio?

   Make a note of any insects found on or near the cactus. Why are they there?

   Finally, find a dead Saguaro on the ground. Examine its rib structure. How does it adjust to heavy rain? To strong winds? How can children determine the strength of the ribs? Of the roots?

The majestic Saguaro cactus. What can be learned about it by observation?

4. *Other Desert Plants* (Intermediate and Upper). Activities similar to the above can be done with such desert plants as Cholla, Barrel Cactus, Hedgehog Cactus, Ironwood, Palo Verde and Creosote Bushes.

   The following general factors can be observed and records or sketches made for later follow-up work in the classroom:

   a. Location, height, color and shape.
   b. Root systems.
   c. Type and number of spines.
   d. Structure of cactus skeletons.
   e. Insects and birds present.
   f. Likenesses and differences.
   g. How protected from the sun.
   h. How adopted to conserve water.
   i. Presence of flowers and seeds.
   j. Leaf or needle structure.

C. *Animals*. The main types of animals that will be found in the desert during the day are insects and their relatives (spiders and scorpions). More difficult to study are birds, rodents and mammals because they normally stay away from people and in the shade or in holes during the day. Some possible activities are as follows:

1. *Ant Dams* (Intermediate and Upper). Find an ant nest. If it is one that has a large ring of plant debris around it, this can provide an interesting inquiry. What caused the ring? How did it get there? What are the particles it is made from?

Ant nest with ring debris around it. This provides many opportunities for inquiry.

Are ants carrying things out or into the nest from the ring? For what possible reasons could the ants be putting the ring there? Activities can be carried out to test children's guesses. (i.e., finding out where the debris comes from, digging into the nest, putting water onto the debris). What effect does the debris have on the runoff of the water? (It is most likely that the debris is used to prevent water runoff and flooding of the nest).

2. *Ant Habits* (Intermediate and Upper). Observe the ants in their nest. Are they all doing the same thing? What are they doing?

Describe the nest: size, shape, special features. Estimate how many ants live in an ant hill or nest.

Are all ants the same size? How far do the ants travel to get their food? How long does each journey take? What do they do with the food? (What is the food?) Compare the weight of an ant with its load (use drinking straw, balanced on a needle).

If ants are not active in a nest try blowing gently into the hole or pour a little water into the hole. Why do ants come out when you do either of these?

Have students try experiments of their own. For instance, what happens if you put an obstacle in the ants way? Does the ant like any other food? How do ants greet each other? What happens when a red and a black ant meet each other? What is the difference between red and black ants? What else do you notice and want to find out about ants?

3. *Termites* (Intermediate and Upper). Where do they live? Always in similar places? Sketch and describe characteristics of nests. Can you find what this is made of? What do they live on? Will they eat anything else? How do they move? How fast? Examine a termite under a hand lens. Sketch details.

    How do termites differ from ants? Put a few termites with nest material in a vial. Notice their activities.

4. *Ground Spiders* (Intermediate and Upper). Describe and sketch their webs. What does the web feel like? What's the temperature in its hole? What are the spiders special features? What has the spider eaten? Can you entice it out? How does it get its moisture?

5. *Black Widow* (Intermediate and Upper). It is not safe to put your hand in its nest. Use a stick after you have observed the nest—if you want to dislodge the spider.

    What kind of web does it have? What does it feel like? How is it different from the nest of the ground spider? What has the black widow eaten? What is the nest like at the entrance? Can you get a glimpse of the spider to estimate its size? Its color? Its speed of movement?

6. *Animal Homes* (All Grade Levels). Choose a small area of about two square meters per group of three to five students. These could be in different desert terrains. Introduce the idea that every living thing has a home and that these homes are designed to meet the special life styles of the individual creatures. Tell students they have 15 minutes to find as many animal homes as they can. Have them sketch the homes they find.

    Regroup and have sketches shared. Estimate the size and type of animals that live there. Does the home help the animal catch food? How? How and of what is the home constructed? How does the animal get in and out? Is there an entrance and exit?

D. *Soils and Rocks*

1. *Rock Count* (Intermediate and Upper). Have students collect rocks from as many different places as possible (flat ground, wash, under trees). By count and observation determine the *native rock*. Do children have examples of rocks in their collections that are not native? How did these get there?

     Have students classify the rocks in some way. Examine the rocks with a hand lens to assist in the observations.

2. *Soil Samples* (Intermediate and Upper). Have students collect soil samples from different places in the desert and at different depths. Make a soil profile. Find the range of soil temperatures on the surface and at different depths. Have students graph their results.

3. *Soil Porosity and Floods* (Intermediate and Upper). Deserts are noted for their flash floods. Why is this? The answer may be in the ability of the soil to absorb or not absorb moisture.

     To test the porosity (ability to take in water), cut both ends out of a one pound coffee can. Locate several locations in the desert: wash, flat ground and under a tree. At each location, insert the can about one inch into the soil. Quickly fill the can with water and measure the time it takes for the water to run out of the can and into the soil. What do the results suggest about flash floods occurring in the desert?

E. *Debris*

1. *Natural Debris* (Any Grade Level)

    a. Have students make a collection of all the dead vegetation and animals they can find. Can they guess the causes of death. (Be careful not to handle insects or animals that are still decaying).

    b. Sort the collection in any ways they wish and make a diagram of their methods. Are there other ways to sort the same objects? Can other uses of the debris be suggested?

    c. In the classroom a display of the collection can be made. How long will the debris last? How could the life of the decaying things be shortened? Lengthened?

    d. Study the items carefully for insect life. What made the insect choose these habitats? How does it live? What are its principle activities? Look at the insects under a hand lens. Make sketches of details.

2. *Man-Made Debris* (Intermediate and Upper). Do all the above activities and the following:

    a. What is the most popular drink? What else can you say about litterbugs? Were they adults or children? What are their preferences? How did the debris get there?

    b. Which kinds of debris could be reprocessed? Could you suggest ways in which the debris could be useful in school or at home? Sketch your ideas.

Note

1. E.F. Adolph and Associates, *Physiology of Man in the Desert,* 1947.

Chapter 9

Activities for Any Site

Introduction

Many of the activities in this chapter either help children organize information they collect or suggest possible ways of combining left and right brain functions to produce creative forms of expression. These also provide the vehicles for integrating the language arts, mathematics, reading, physical education and the fine arts into curriculum. To help provide suggestions of the many possible modes of expression that can be used by children to follow-up outdoor activities, the following flow diagram is presented.

Any Site Flow Chart

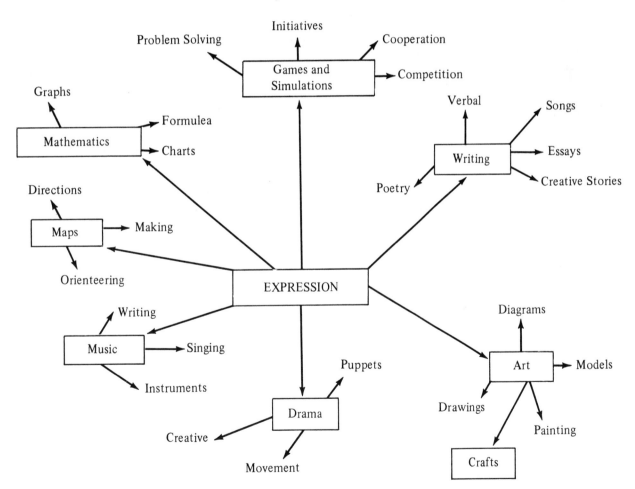

I. **Mathematics**

Most of the activities in this book require children to collect a variety of information. Examples of some of the ways this data can be recorded and displayed are as follows:

A. *Tabular Form,* e.g.,

Where Found

Name of Insect	On Saguaro	In Ground	On Cholla
Bee Fly	X		
Ground Spider		X	
Black Widow		X	X

B. *Graphing*

Bar or Count Graph   *Population Count*

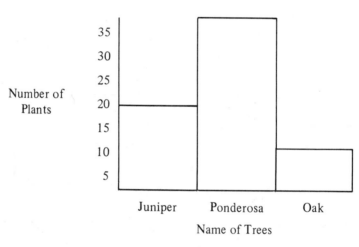

Which trees occurred most often?
Least often?
Arrange in order.

2. *Temperature Graph.* These are often drawn as continuous graphs. Over a short time, this probably gives a true picture.

e.g., Continuous graphs (point graphs)

Table

Distance from Rock Fall (inches)	Temperature (degrees F)
0	80
2	75
4	71
6	69

Graph

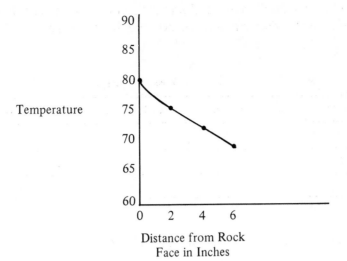

Temperature

Distance from Rock
Face in Inches

C. *Random Sampling Techniques* (Intermediate and Upper). The two techniques described below permit children to study an environmental area in an organized way. They help students determine approximate numbers of organisms living in a given area. They also help students learn to work together on a common problem.

1. *Line Transect.* Stand in the middle of the study area selected by the teacher with a compass and randomly select a degree reading. Then draw a line (or use string to lay out in a line) to represent this direction across the entire study area. This line can be marked on a map of the study area.

    This line represents a sample representative of the total area. Children can then determine the following:

    a. How many different kinds of plants touch the line? (Consider the line to be a vertical plane extending up beyond the highest point.)
    b. What is the percentage of the different kinds of plants found? Do you think this is representative of the total area of the study? How many different line transects would you need to be accurate?
    c. What is the percentage of ground covered by the different plants along the line transect? Is there a difference between density of plants and number of plants?
    d. Record your results in some way.
    e. The same procedure could be used for determining approximate numbers of insects and other animals (including evidence of animals).
    f. Additional information such as temperature, soil porosity, pH, type of soil, etc., could also be gathered along the line transect.

2. *Quadrant Study.* The total study area selected by the teacher could be considered a series of connecting one-square meter segments. Each of these could be considered a sample of the whole area. To select a sample square or quadrant have students throw

Quandrant Study. The quandrant these boys selected in a city park includes a large tree.

a rock over their shoulder into the study area (random selection). Where it lands the students mark off a square meter area with string. This quadrant can also be placed on a map of the entire study area.

Children observe and record as many living organisms in this area as possible. (Or factors related to temperature, sun light, soil porosity, ph, type of soil, etc., can be measured). Children can determine if they wish to consider areas above and below the ground. If so, how far?

Different quadrants can be selected and similar investigations conducted. What are the differences and similarities? Why?

Follow up questions might be:

a.   What living things were found?

b.   How are they related?

c.   Is there evidence that man has started or thwarted erosion in the study area?

II. **Maps** (Intermediate and Uppers)

Children are capable of making fairly accurate maps of the regions in which they do their activities. Once complete, the map can be used to designate specific areas where children are to collect data. Data collected (i.e., animal homes, plants, temperatures, etc.) can then be recorded for later reference on the map.

Room does not permit identification of all the possible methods children can use to create maps. However, it has been proven that if you arm small groups of children with string, rulers, sighting devices for determining angles (and the know how to use these) children will usually come up with all the appropriate aspects of a "good" map including use of scale, keys, symbols and directions. Once a variety of maps have been created, the class can determine those aspects of making maps that all should use in order to communicate effectively with one another.

III. **Music**

A. *Instruments.* Children can collect containers, tubes, debris, rocks with holes, cactus needles, reeds, acorns, etc., as part of their outdoor activities. Many of these can be made into musical instruments with a little imagination.

B. *Singing Songs.* Singing in the outdoors serves several purposes including the creation of feelings of friendship and fellowship. Usually singing follows a format which includes one or two introductory songs familiar to all in order to warm the group. This can be followed by the introduction of new songs, singing in the round, singing games or stories. Then after this fairly boisterous period two or three quieter songs can be sung to prepare for bedtime.

C. *Creating Songs and Music.*

1. While many songs serve as a socialization experience, songs with verses that can be created by children can serve to recap events of the day or trip. The song "Old Mac-Donald" can be sung about the camp using camp creatures rather than farm animals. The song "Oh You Can't Get to Heaven" allows many opportunities for students to have fun with the events of camp.

2. Using a familiar tune ("Mary Had a Little Lamb," "Row, Row, Row your Boat") make up a song using the natural features of the environment you're in.

3. Divide the class into groups of five. Explain that many years ago they would not have had the musical instruments that we have now. If that was so, what would be some of the things that could be used to make the noise for music? Have each group go off by themselves and come up with a short musical skit depicting music that could have been made years ago.

4. Ask the children to sit quietly and listen to the sounds of *nature*. Have them describe and discuss these nature sounds. Talk about man-made sounds. What is the source of these sounds? Imitate a natural sound. Imitate the man-made sounds. Act them out to a tune of one of their favorite songs using the sounds instead of the words.

D. *Song Games.*

1. Charades—divide group into teams. Each team acts out in pantomime the title of a song that is familiar to the group. Guessers must sing the song they think is being dramatized.

2. Song contest—divide group into teams. Leader of one group calls a subject; competing team must respond within a few seconds with a song pertinent to the subject. If they can't, the challenging group must sing one. Examples:

   a. Color—Lavender's Blue, Green Grow the Rushes
   b. Rivers—Swanee, Shenandoah
   c. Girl's names—Sandy, Marianina
   d. Transportation—Erie Canal, Bicycle Built for Two

IV. **Language Arts**

Many forms of poetry can be developed by children as a result of activities in the outdoors provided the experiences encourage children to use language in connection with textures, sounds, shapes, and feelings. Some of the simpler forms of poetry are as follows:

A. *Haiku,* originated by the Japanese, consists of three lines of five, seven, and five syllables each. The emphasis is syllabic, not rhyming. Example:

> The snow covered tree
> Sparkles in the soft moonlight
> The wind rushes by

B. *Cinquain* is derived from the French and Spanish words for five. This form of poetry also is based on syllables but their are five lines. Each line has a mandatory purpose and number of syllables. These are (a) the title in two syllables, (b) description of the title in four syllables, (c) description of action in six syllables, (d) description of a feeling in eight syllables, and (5) another word for the title in two syllables. Example:

> Balloons
> Graceful, growing
> Climbing among the clouds
> Joyfully stalking the sunset
> Alive.

A simpler version of Cinquain is to ignore the syllables and have the right number of words per line. Structure is thus:

Line 1—One word that identifies the subject or title
Line 2—Two words that explain the title
Line 3—Three words that show action
Line 4—Four words that complete line three
Line 5—One word which also explains the title.

Example:

> Stream
> Cool, clear
> Running, rocky, rapids
> refreshing, rewarding, fresh, fulfilling
> water

C. *Diamante* is a poem shaped in the form of a diamond that demonstrates that words are related through shades of meaning from one extreme to the opposite extreme. For example, "life" and "death."

> Life
> green, bright
> shining, growing, blooming
> heat, motion, soul, grave
> fading, slowing, dimming
> brown, old
> death

The words chosen should match the following pattern of parts of speech:

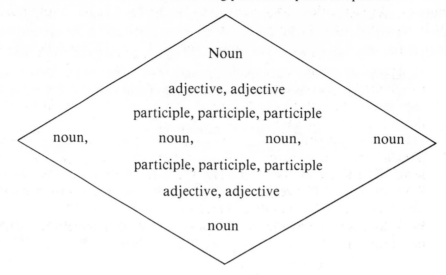

Noun

adjective, adjective

participle, participle, participle

noun,   noun,   noun,   noun

participle, participle, participle

adjective, adjective

noun

D.   *Visualizing Words*. Words or phrases can be printed out so that something in the design relates to the meaning of the word or phrase. Some words that lend themselves to this kind of picture word play are:

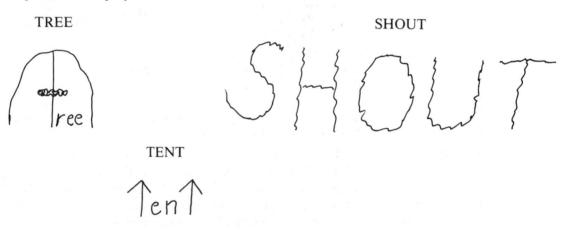

TREE

SHOUT

TENT

E.   Other worthwhile language arts activities besides poetry are as follows:

1.   Daily log or diary (good for resident camp situation). One page can be used for each day to indicate: "What I did in the morning," "What I did in the afternoon," "What I did in the evening," and "My thoughts of what I did (observations, feelings, drawings)."
2.   Creating song books of songs that can be sung at camp.
3.   Creative writing. Children write stories as though they were the plant, rock, animal, etc., they are investigating. Stories can tell how the object got there, how it "feels" to be that object, how it interacts with other objects and what will happen to it in the future.
4.   Story Telling. Again children can make up stories to tell about outdoor events or things. One excellent way to do this is to tell the class Indian Legends or Greek Myths about how the stars got in the sky. Children can then pick out their own groups of stars and make up their own legends or myths to explain how the stars got there.
5.   Group Story. At a spot in the outdoors that particularly sparks the imagination, let the group make up a story. You could start it off, then let each person add something to the story.

V. **Arts and Crafts**

Some specific suggestions have been given in previous chapters. Additional suggestions which can be modified for most environments are as follows:

A. Collect natural materials in a variety of colors and display them on a large bulletin board. If the students gather these during a class walk, it offers an opportunity to discuss conservation practices in collecting. Help students develop some classifications (such as natural, man-made, beautiful, ugly); classify the materials and explain why they placed each material in a certain category.

B. Students may use natural materials to create a mobile, collage, or scene.

C. Students may make crayon rubbings or charcoal rubbings (with burnt wood) using various textured natural materials such as bark, leaves, seeds, rocks, and sand.

D. Students may use leaves, dried seeds, ferns, and other natural materials to create forest creatures (real or imaginary) and then name them.

E. Students may glue acorns, nuts, cones, and similar materials together to make "seed" people or animals.

Acorn

Pine Cone

Maple Seeds

F. Students may use natural materials dipped in paint to make designs. For instance, roll paint-covered pinecones over paper to make prints.

G. Students may make a design on dark paper. First apply glue to paper, then shake on sand, soil, or crushed materials. Allow to dry completely before displaying.

H. Students make leaf prints leading to classification activities: crayon rubbings or spatter prints (using paint and toothbrush) or ink pad prints can be used.

I. Draw something from an ant's (or any small animal) eye view.

J. Paper weights can be made of a rock that is decorated with paint, glue and dirt, pine needles and covered with shellac.

K. Weavings can be made using cardboard or twigs as loom; put notch along top and bottom—evenly spaced. Then use string or yarn and stretch from top to bottom and wrap around each notch—this is the wrap. To weave the woof—use yarn, twigs, leaves, anything to make an interesting design.

VI. Games

A. *Activities for Bus or Car*

1. *Mile Pole Observation* (Intermediate and Upper). A great deal can be learned about the life zones of a region if you are driving great distances through different zones. One way to collect information is by making and recording observations of what is seen out the car or bus window as you travel along.

   Here's how. All state highways have mile pole markers every mile which usually indicate the distance remaining to the end of the highway or state border. Once on the highway, locate a mile pole. Record the mile number on the chart which follows. Then make the additional observations asked for on the chart. Repeat this procedure every five miles. Every so often review your observations and make comparisons. The questions below will assist in these comparisons.

   For observation purposes, children should attempt to view the environment only from their own side of the car or bus.

   Questions

   a. How does what is observed from one side of the road compare with the other side of the road.

   b. If there are differences, what could be the causes?

   c. How has man influenced the types of vegetation and wildlife observed at each location?

   d. What are the major changes in the kinds of plant life observed and recorded? Where did these occur? What could be possible causes?

   e. A cross-section chart could be made showing elevation differences and the kinds of plants found at each mile pole observation point.

Mile Pole Observation Form

Mile Post	% of Land Covered by Trees	Predominant Type of Vegetation	Height of Predominant Vegetation	Avg. Dist. between Vegetation	Wildlife Seen	Evidence of Man (pole, fence, house)	Approx. Altitude*
1.							
2.							
3.							
4.							
5.							
6.							
7.							
8.							
9.							
10.							
11.							
12.							
13.							
14.							
15.							
16.							
17.							
18.							
19.							
20.							

*Can be found on most road maps.

2. *Written and Verbal Activities* (Intermediate and Upper). Those that take up time and lessen boredom while on trips:

   a. *Buried Bird Sentences*. Within these sentences are the names of birds. Underline the name of bird which is ''buried.'' Can be done individually or in teams.

     (1) The wolves h*owl*ed at midnight.
     (2) It takes a brave bandit to *rob in* daylight.
     (3) *Do v*entilate the new house better.
     (4) This pencil is a hal*f-inch* longer.
     (5) You can't *kill deer* without a license.
     (6) The boy left the porch wit*h awk*ard strides.
     (7) The wind*ow l*ooks over the garden.
     (8) He saw them bo*th rush* down the valley.
     (9) Her eye*s wan*dered over the curious crowd.
     (10) The *crow*n lay shattered on the granite floor.

   b. *Scrambled Bird Names* (You could do this for any outdoor idea).

     (1) obbthiew—bobwhite
     (2) ahkwtihgn—nighthawk
     (3) aprswor—sparrow
     (4) ceedkooprw—woodpecker
     (5) hhrstu—thrush
     (6) aecukpssr—sapsucker
     (7) cjnou—junco
     (8) abbcdiklr—blackbird

   c. *What Letter of the Alphabet is it?* What letter is:

     (1) an insect? _____ (B)
     (2) a body of water? _____ (C)
     (3) a command to a horse? _____ (G)
     (4) In the head? _____ (I)
     (5) Is a bird? _____ (J)
     (6) Part of a house? _____ (L)
     (7) a spring vegetable? _____ (P)
     (8) an actor's signal? _____ (Q)
     (9) a beverage? _____ (T)
     (10) a sheep? _____ (U)

3. *Outdoor Analogies*. Here are a few of the possibilities that you or children could create:

   a. Insect is to six as spider is to (1) two (2) four (3) *eight* (4) 100
   b. Bird is to feathers as fish is to (1) fins (2) claws (3) gills (4) *scales*
   c. Tadpole is to frog as caterpillar is to (1) goose (2) *butterfly* (3) frog (4) fish
   d. Sky is to blue as grass is to (1) rainbow (2) blew (3) snake (4) *green*
   e. Tree is to bark as body is to (1) voice (2) *skin* (3) hands (4) height

4. *Nature's Inventors*. Many modern inventions were derived from abilities or habits of animals. Try matching the animal with the invention.

a.	Bat (5)	1. gun blasts and chemical attack
b.	Armodillo (6)	2. anesthesia
c.	Chameleon (10)	3. electricity
d.	Deep-sea fishes (3)	4. parachute
e.	Squid (7)	5. sonar
f.	Flying squirrel (4)	6. tank
g.	Hummingbird (11)	7. jet propulsion
h.	Birds (9)	8. hypodermic
i.	Scorpion (8)	9. plane flaps
j.	Snake (2)	10. camouflage
k.	Beetle (1)	11. helicopter

B. *Group Initiatives.* These can be used as ice-breakers and aids for getting acquainted. Processes of physical contact, communication and team effort are required. They also permit the instructor as well as the group to observe individual strengths in leadership and personality of the participants. Finally, these types of activities help to develop an awareness of decision making, leadership and obligations of individuals to the group.

Some initiations that require no "hardware" and can be set up anywhere are:

1. *Animal Lineup.* Whisper names of different animals to each participant. Using only the sounds that animal makes, the group will arrange itself in order by size.

2. *The Monster.* The members of the group must join themselves together and walk with both hands and feet on the ground as one single "monster," for some distance. The number of feet that can touch the ground is one more than 1/2 the number of participants. The number of hands is equal to 1/2 the number of participants. With youngsters, try 1/2N feet and N hands where N equals the number in the group.

3. *Acid Factory Accident.* There has been an accident in an acid factory and the acid is all over the floor and the group is to decide how to get out of the factory without stepping on the acid. To assist them, the group should have one less paper plate than there are people in the group. If a person falls into the acid, they can be fished out to continue crossing, but their paper plate is lost. The entire group is to cross the acid covered floor for a distance of some twenty yards and once a person is "safe" he/she may not return to the starting point.

VII. **Process Activities**

A. *Stone Identification* (Any Grade Level). Ask each student fo find a stone. Sitting cross-legged in a circle, have each person get to know their rock by feeling its shapes, indentations, textures, etc. Give them a minute or two to do this. Then ask everyone to pass their stones to you. After jumbling them up, have students close their eyes; then begin to pass the stones, one at a time, around the circle. Each time a child receives a stone he/she will feel it to see if it is his/hers. When they think they have their stone, they can let it drop to the ground, open their eyes and continue passing any other stones that are passed to them.

B. *Which Way Did They Go?* (Intermediate and upper). This is an activity designed to involve children in the processes of observing critically, giving directions or reporting observations and following directions. These skills have tremendous carry over value in the entire curriculum as well as in every day life.

Directions:

1. Have children work in teams of three. Each team will need a portable tape recorder and knowledge of how to use it.
2. Their task is to walk off in some direction. As they walk they report into the tape what they are observing. If they know how to use a compass and estimate distances, they can include this information on the tape as well.
3. Keep walking at least for 15 minutes until they find some interesting object like a tree, evidence of animal, bird nest, rock, anything. Without telling the name of the object, list as many observations as possible about the object into the tape recorder.
4. Return to the original starting spot and exchange tape recorders with another group and see if they can follow their path and find and identify the other group's object at the end of the tape.
5. Repeat with another group's tape until time is out.
6. Save the last 15 minutes to discuss such things as:

    a. What kinds of directions were easy to follow?
    b. Which were hard to follow?
    c. What's the difference between an observation and an inference? Were any of the observations really inferences? Did inference statements make it harder, easier or no difference in finding directions?
    d. Others.

C. *Environmental Communications* (Any Grade Level). Not only are students communicating with one another about the environment and to the environment, but the environment is communicating to them as well.

Have children look and listen to the environment. What kinds of communications are there? There should be communications which are audible as well as non-verbal, animal as well as human, and from living and non-living objects.

Questions: How many ways can you pick up environmental communications (seeing, hearing, touching, smelling, tasting)?

How many different feelings do the physical perceptions of the environment convey to the aware observer (pleasure, joy, thoughtfullness, sadness, fear, hope)?

How many different sounds can be heard on the site? How are they alike? How are they different? How can they be identified? What emotions do they suggest?

Do inanimate (vegetable and mineral) objects in the environment communicate with us? How?

What danger signals can you read from the environment which tell you the land has been misused?

Action. Now have the children go off by themselves into the environment without talking to anyone else. They should walk for awhile, sit for awhile, walk again, all the time allowing the environment to communicate with them. When about 30–45 minutes have passed, signal the students to return and have them share in small groups their impressions and communications.

The solo hiking experience offers opportunities to communicate with the outdoors and with oneself.

D. *Memory Circle*. (Intermediate and Upper). A good way to recap the events of several outdoor activities in a particular environment is to play this memory circle game.

Arrange your students in a circle. The first child will tell something they observed or did in the forest (or at water, desert, city, school site). The next player repeats the first statement and adds one of his own. The game continues around the circle until everyone has a turn or until the list is too long to remember.

A follow-up activity of this would be to list student's statements and then ask the class to decide if each observation or action was beneficial, detrimental, or had little effect on the environment.

Discussion questions to guide might be:

1. What makes an action or observation beneficial?
2. How do we distinguish between a detrimental and a beneficial effect?
3. Were any of the actions detrimental to the environment but beneficial to people? Can we justify such actions? How? When?
4. Were any actions detrimental to people but beneficial to the environment? Can we justify these actions? How? When?

Concluding Thought
from Both Brains

A DISCOVERY

A small child looks up
  with "simple" whys.
He is given "the answer,"
  did you notice his eyes?
Have you really given him something
  or have you taken it away?

The "spark" and the "whys" are there
  when he comes to you—
Is it just answers he needs
  or more questions too?

Do you answer honestly
  "I don't know, let's learn together,"
Or should only the student be learning
  the answers you already know?

What kindles the excitement with you,
  a list of "right" answers
Or his question—"What else can I do"?

He is discovering—must he stop now?
  He must go to math,
Or is the math here somehow?

Outside the school these are together
  the music, math, art, and weather,
Perhaps it's o.k. to learn that way too
  or—could it be better?

They come to us
  with so many "why's,"
Let's stop dispensing answers
  and look into their eyes.

by
Mary Christen
Elementary School Teacher
Mesa, Arizona
Summer—1978

Appendices

Appendix A

(School District)

Letter to Parents

Dear Parent:

The school district is proud to announce that _____ School will again be able to provide an outdoor education learning experience for your child.

_____ School has been a pioneer school for outdoor education in the district. Thirty students attended Camp Tontozona, as a district pioneer project in 1973. Last year an impossible task was accomplished when two learning centers raised enough money to rent buses and station wagons to take *225 students* to Morman Lake, Arizona.

The school district has granted through TRI-FUND over $1,000 to the school outdoor education program called VENTURE OUT. The program written by teachers of the school is for the purchase of educational and recreational equipment to be used both at school and at camp. Both teachers are currently teaching for Arizona State University; the course is "Outdoor Education for Teachers."

The time spent at the Lake Pleasant Outdoor Education Center can be one of the high spots of your child's educational experience. It is a carefully planned learning project that cannot be duplicated in the classroom. Conservation, the value of our watersheds and resources may be learned in their natural setting. Democratic group living at the camp affords opportunities for healthful living, character development, and social adjustment which can rarely be found elsewhere.

PLACE: Lake Pleasant Outdoor Education Center-Lower Lake

SUPERVISION: 4 classroom teachers. 12 Thunderbird High School Honor Students.

COST—3 DAYS: $8.50 covers: Room rental, transportation costs, insurance costs, counselor fee, and all food costs.

FACILITIES: 5 large white buildings are sleeping quarters. They are divided into sleeping units of 12 each with a bathroom with a shower. 1 large administration building that includes classrooms, dining area and kitchen.

INSURANCE: The students are covered by *CNA Insurance*. The pink form explains the full coverage.

White form must be completed and returned or student can't go.

This form stays with the camp nurse—any medication must be turned into the homeroom teacher 2 days before leaving.

TIME: Wednesday, February 12, 1979: Students arrive as usual at 8:30. They bring sack lunch and sleeping bag with clothes. 10:30. Leave for Outdoor Education Facility.

Thursday, February 13, 1979: Students at school camp.

Friday, February 14, 1979: Students arrive at school, eat lunch at school—films, and valentine party.

Appendix B

Permission and Registration Form

(School District)

STUDENT'S NAME _____   Telephone _____

_Listed _Unlisted

Home Address _____

Name of Father _____   Business Telephone _____

Name of Mother _____   Business Telephone _____

Name of responsible adult who will assume responsibility for
child if parents cannot be reached:

Name _____

Address _____   Telephone _____

Family Physician _____   Telephone _____

Address _____

I grant permission for my child to attend the Outdoor Education Center at Lake Pleasant.

DATE _____   _____

Signature of Parent

****

Does your child have any physical limitations?   ____Yes ____No
   Comment on type:

Does your child have any allergies?   ____Yes ____No
   Comment on type:

Is your child under a doctor's care at this date   ____Yes ____No
   Comment:

Is your child taking any type of medicine?   ____Yes ____No
   Comment:

Does your child walk or talk in his sleep?   ____Yes ____No

Has your child had a tetanus shot? ____Yes ____No

Has your child had any major illnesses in the last year? ____Yes ____No
Comment:

If there are any suggestions which you think might help your child at Lake Pleasant Center, please comment below.

Appendix C

Medical Form
(School District)

To be filled in by the parent or guardian. Failure to return this completed record to the school will not permit the camper's enrollment in the camp program.

Name _____ Sex_____ Birth Date _____

Address _____

Person to be contacted in case of emergency _____

Address _____ Telephone _____

Father and/or Mother's place of employment:

Name _____ Address _____ Telephone _____

Name _____ Address _____ Telephone _____

In case of emergency, I understand every effort will be made to contact me.
In the event I cannot be reached, I hereby give permission to the physician selected by the camp director to hospitalize and secure proper treatment (including surgery) for my child.

Date _____ Signature of parent or guardian _____

The above-names may participate fully in the camp's program and activities excepting _____

Date _____ Signature of parent or guardian _____

Name of family doctor _____

I authorize the teachers to administer aspirin, alka seltzer, pepto bismol or similar non-perscription medication according to recommended dosages if needed.

Date _____ Signature of parent or guardian _____

If prescription medication is to be administered, please secure a district Nurse's form #16 to have your doctor complete.

If there is any question of your child's health, please secure a physician's examination. If your child is in normal health, please fill out the following information:

Date of last immunization from: Tetanus _____ Diptheria _____ Polio _____

Smallpox _____ Whooping cough _____ Measles _____ .

Past history of serious lacerations, injuries or illnesses: _____

_____

_____

Allergies _____

Penicillin or other drug reactions _____

Special medication or dietary routine _____

_____

****

To be used by camp health person during camp.

Date _____ Complaint _____ Treatment _____

_____

_____

_____

_____

Appendix D

Outdoor Education Student's Checklist

This is a guideline checklist for a camping experience from 1–5 days. Make your own checklist fit your needs according to weather, time of year, and length of trip.

ALL BELONGINGS SHOULD BE MARKED

Sleeping Equipment

_____ bedroll or sleeping bag

Clothing

_____ night clothes

_____ long pants

_____ shirts

_____ underwear

_____ socks

_____ sweater or sweatshirt

_____ heavy jacket

_____ hat

_____ shoes—1 heavy pair, 1 pair tennis shoes

_____ rain gear

Items for Health and Cleanliness

_____ soap

_____ towel and washcloth

_____ stiff comb and hairbrush

_____ toothbrush and toothpaste

_____ shampoo

_____ suntan lotion

_____ deodorant

_____ plastic bag for soiled clothes

Equipment

_____ gloves

_____ canteen or plastic bottle

_____ cup (plastic or tin)

_____ flashlight

_____ camera

_____ ballpoint pens or pencils

_____ sack lunch

Suggested Items *NOT* to bring

_____ money

_____ radio

_____ knives

_____ shorts

_____ sandals

_____ cowboy boots

_____ purses

_____ jewelry

_____ snacks, gum, sunflower seeds

Suggested Uncommon Items for Teacher to have

_____ spare shoe laces

_____ pencils or pens and small pencil sharpener

_____ matches

_____ knife

_____ masking tape

_____ string-nylon

Appendix E

Lake Pleasant Schedule

(Sample
Schedule)

Monday

8:30	Check in. Collect foil dinners and lunches
	Collect lunch money
	Discuss whistle call and buddy system
	Discuss camp arrival procedure
9:00	Take luggage to loading zone
9:30	Bus arrival
11:00	Arrive at lake. Unload bus, inventory facilities. Free outdoor time.
12:00	Sack lunch.
12:30	Large group lecture over topographical maps and environment. Break into groups of 2 for observation of small area
1:45	Discussion
2:15	Break
2:30	Break into groups A. Orienteering
	B. Oddities of Nature and Survival
	C. Water life
4:30	Free time
5:30	Bunks
6:00	Supper
6:30	Bunks (clean-up crew in kitchen)
7:00	Campfire activities
9:00	Go to cabins to work on skits for Tuesday
9:30	Clean-up of selves and cabins
10:00	Lights out (quiet talking o.k.)
10:30	To sleep. There is a six mile hike tomorrow.

Tuesday

6:00	Cooks up. Breakfast crew
6:30	Everyone up. Wash and take care of cabins before coming to breakfast.
7:00	Breakfast Group A
7:15	Breakfast Group B
7:30	Breakfast Group C

7:45	Bunks (clean-up crew in kitchen)
8:15	Prepare for hike to dam
8:30	Depart
10:30	Dam tour
11:30	Return hike
12:30	Arrive at camp, rest in bunks. Cooks for lunch in kitchen.
1:00	Lunch
1:30	Bunks (clean-up crew in kitchen)
3:00	Break into Groups A, B, C
3:15	Switch groups
5:00	Free time (cooks in kitchen)
5:30	Bunks
6:00	Supper
6:30	Bunks (clean-up crew in kitchen)
7:00	Campfire (skits, singing)
9:30	Cabins
10:00	Lights out
10:30	Sleep

Wednesday

6:00	Cooks up
6:30	Group up
6:30–7:00	Cabin inspection. All gear must be packed and set outside the door. Teacher will come to section and excuse you to breakfast. All gear to be piled up by the barbeque before going inside to eat. You will eat as you are passed on inspection. Those with the cleanest rooms will eat first.
8:00	Classes—wrap-up of what has been learned at Lake Pleasant
	Back to school
12:30	Eat lunch at cafeteria

Appendix F

Rules

Bus Rules—Cafeteria Rules—Dorm Rules

Bus

1. Line up before getting on bus.
2. Stay in seat when bus is moving.
3. Keep hands, arms, legs, head inside the bus.
4. No food or drink on bus. No gum, sunflower seeds, candy, etc. Water is permitted.
5. Singing is permitted—yelling is not.
6. When leaving bus, the front rows file out first.
7. Keep all luggage out of aisle.
8. Soft luggage is preferred (it packs better).
9. Help teachers take a head count before getting on the bus.
10. Be courteous to the bus driver, teachers and aides.
11. If an emergency comes up, notify a teacher or aide immediately.

CAFETERIA

1. Dress appropriately—shoes, shirts, etc.
2. Be on time for meals. Meals are not served late.
3. Take only what you will eat.
4. Don't take food from the eating area.
5. Don't yell or play during meals.
6. Be on time for cooking or clean-up duty.

DORM AND CAMP

1. Lights out at 10:00 P.M.
2. All luggage goes under the bottom bunk.
3. Straighten up your area before breakfast.
4. Clean up after yourself—don't expect anyone to wait on you.
5. Be in your bunk 1/2 hour before and/or after each meal.
6. Don't bring valuables such as radios, tape recorder, etc.
7. No gum.
8. Don't collect items near camp.
9. No running at any time.

MORE CAFETERIA RULES

1. Use polite table manners at all times.
2. Wash hands before eating.
3. Don't touch or take other people's food.

174

4. Be quiet while eating.

5. Don't take cuts or push in line.

6. Be helpful . . . help clean up the area where you eat. Push in your chair after eating.

7. Be a good worker when working on K.P. duty.

8. Only after you've finished cleaning your plate should you go for seconds. Take only what you can eat.

Appendix G

Sample Check Sheet For Monitoring Children's Activities

These are only sample items. Actual check sheets should reflect the goals and objectives of a particular unit and be suitable for children's levels of abilities.

The types of items identified below could be set up on a large check sheet allowing room for each child's name or a separate sheet could be developed for each child. An example of a check sheet that could be used for an individual child is provided below. Whether the sheet is for a whole class or an individual child, recording symbols such as the following can be used:

H	= High	•	= Satisfactory
M	= Medium or	X	= Check again
L	= Low	·	= Give special attention

Note that these symbols have the advantage of being changed easily after a child gives evidence of progress.

It is not necessary or recommended that check sheets be used with every activity. Record observations as they come to your attention, without "testing" your pupils consciously in this respect. If you find this loose structure too easy to remember, then you can either:

a. Select certain children to concentrate on for each lesson or
b. Predetermine which lessons you use to run a check on each child.

In either case it should not be necessary to monitor each child more than four times a year on each of the items on your check sheet.

A. *Use of Knowledge*   (General Items)[1]

◯ 1. Can the child tell you in clear concise language what he/she is doing during an activity?
◯ 2. When you are describing and/or experimenting, does the child use the information he/she has gathered, rather than what he/she thinks the answer is?
◯ 3. When the child interprets what an experiment means does he/she rely on the information which the learning activity provided?
◯ 4. Does the child relate ideas from the previous learning activity to the current one?
◯ 5. Etc.

(Specific, in relation to the concept of the life cycle)[2]

◯ 1. Did he/she describe changes in size and structure either of animals in general or of his/her animals?
◯ 2. Could he/she identify animals or pictures that illustrate changes in size and structure?
◯ 3. Did he/she spontaneously use the words egg, larva, pupa, and adult?
◯ 4. Could he/she identify examples of eggs, larvae, pupae, and adults from pictures of living materials?
◯ 5. Etc.

B. *Process Skills*

○ 1. Is the child able to formulate questions or problems from available observations?

○ 2. Does the child record, in some way, the information she/he gets from an activity?

○ 3. Is the child able to make guesses (or inferences or hypothesis) to explain observations or answer questions?

○ 4. Etc.

C. *Social Skills*

○ 1. Does the child talk with other children about their work?

○ 2. Is the child charitable and open in dialoging with ideas with which they do not agree?

○ 3. Does the child listen to others?

○ 4. Does the child share materials and equipment with other children?

○ 5. Etc.

D. *Attitudes* (About Learning)

○ 1. Is the child able to say, "I don't know" with the expectation that they are going to do something about finding out?

○ 2. Does the child exhibit initiative and skill in finding out what they want to know?

○ 3. Can the child afford to make mistakes freely and profit from them?

○ 4. Does the child attempt to express ideas about which they have only vague and intuitive awareness?

○ 5. Is the child able to suspend judgement?

○ 6. Etc.

E. *Interests*

○ 1. Does the child initiate activities that are new to the classroom?

○ 2. Does the child have real interests of their own?

○ 3. Is the child capable of intense involvement? Have they ever had a passionate commitment to anything?

○ 4. Does the child continue to explore things which are not assigned—outside of school as well as within?

○ 5. Is the child self propelled?

○ 6. Is the child inner directed?

○ 7. Etc.

Notes

1. Derived from Dr. John Renner, tape recording "Teaching Science to Children." *Involving the Child in Science,* tape recording, Listener Co. Hollywood, Calif. 1973.
2. Derived from Rita W. Peterson, "Life Cycles Evaluation Supplement", *Science Curriculum Improvement Study,* Lawrence Hall of Science, University of California, Berkely, California, 1972.

Appendix H-1

**Resident Outdoor School Program
Parent Reactions**

School _____

Outdoor Center _____

Dates of
Outdoor School _____

Dear Parent:

Your boy or girl has just returned from a week at our resident outdoor school. The outdoor center was used to provide worthwhile educational experiences which could not be provided as well in any other situation.

We are most interested in your reactions to the outdoor school experience for your child (or children) and in your suggestions for improvement. Your response to the following questions, as well as your general comments, will be most helpful.

_____   _____
Principal   Curriculum Coordinator

1. Had your child been to an outdoor school before?   Yes _____   No _____

2. Would you be willing to send your child again?   Yes _____   No _____
   Why?

3. What are some of the observable outcomes and learnings?

   (a)

   (b)

   (c)

4. What part of the experience do you feel was most valuable?

5. Suggestions and general comments:

_____
Signature of Parent

Date

Appendix H-2

(School District)

**Resident Outdoor School Program
Teacher Reactions**

TO: Teachers Accompanying Students to the Outdoor School

We sincerely hope that the week at the outdoor school was a pleasant experience which contributed to the achievement of the educational objectives of our school system. We would appreciate your frank comments in answer to the following questions, in order to improve the outdoor school program in the future.

_____

Curriculum Coordinator

What did you especially enjoy in the week's experiences?

What didn't you enjoy?

What are some of the values that you feel were gained by the students from their experience?

What suggestions do you have for improvement?

Name and school   _____

Outdoor center   _____

Dates of the
Outdoor School   _____

Appendix H-3

(School District)

Opinion of Classroom Teachers About Changes in Pupil Attitudes
After the Outdoor School Experience

School _____

Outdoor Center   Dates of the
Attended _____   Outdoor School _____

1. Were any of the children more helpful in doing classroom and associated tasks after they returned from the outdoor school? Yes ____ No ____

   Comments: _____

2. Has your group's attitude toward school work changed since the experience? Yes ____ No ____

   Comments: _____

   _____

3. Do your children show an increased interest in the various learning areas?

   Science: Yes ____ No ____

   Communication arts: Yes ____ No ____

   Art: Yes ____ No ____

   Math: Yes ____ No ____

   Social Studies: Yes ____ No ____

   Physical education: Yes ____ No ____

   Music: Yes ____ No ____

   Others:

   Comments: _____

5. In considering the total effect of the week in the outdoor center, do you feel that the experience has been of any value in improving your teaching? Yes ____ No ____

   How? _____

6. As a result of spending a week with your class at the outdoor school, do you note any difference in your understanding or relationship with the class? Yes ____ No ____

   Comments: _____

7. In your opinion, what would be the greatest value derived from the program? _____

_____

8. Have you noticed any change in acceptance of pupils who were usually "left out" previous to the experience? Yes _____ No _____

Comments: _____

9. Did any of the children show great self-reliance after returning? Yes _____ No _____

Comments: _____

_____

10. As a result of their outdoor experience, do pupils seem more considerate of others?

Yes _____ No _____

Comments: _____

11. Did any of the "behavior problems" change for the better after the experience? Had none _____

Yes _____ No _____

Comments: _____

12. What reactions have you had from parents? _____

_____

13. What reactions have you had from children? _____

_____

14. Did children show improvement in health practices after returning from the trip?

Yes _____ No _____ In what ways? _____

15. What changes, if any, does an outdoor school experience cause you to make in your teaching methods? _____

_____

16. What suggestions would you offer to improve the program?

_____

Name (Optional)

Date _____

Appendix H-4

Student Evaluation of the Resident Outdoor School Program

School _____

Today's
Date _____

Dates at the
Outdoor Center _____

Outdoor Center
Attended _____

Student _____

CHOOSE THE STATEMENT IN EACH GROUP THAT COMES CLOSEST TO YOUR THOUGHTS.

Circle one number only

1. The week at the outdoor center was lots of fun. I certainly enjoyed it.
2. I really didn't care much for the week at the center.
3. I had a fairly good time.
4. It was "okay" but I don't know whether I would go again.

Circle One number only

1. I enjoyed the work experiences in connection with meals, keeping the place clean, and other necessary responsibilities.
2. At the outdoor school everyone shares in the duties and I didn't mind helping out.
3. It wasn't any fun at all to work at our outdoor school.

Circle one number only

1. Since our outdoor school experience, I feel that I am getting along better with the people in my class.
2. I really don't know whether the experience has made any difference in the friendliness of our class.
3. After we came back, I feel our class is even friendlier with each other.
4. I don't think that the outdoor experience made any difference in the friendliness of our class.

Circle one number only

1. My parents thought that the outdoor school experience was good for me.
2. I don't know what my parents think about the outdoor school.
3. I don't think my parents would care to have me go again.

Circle one number only

1. It would be more fun if the sixth grade teacher didn't have to go along on the trip.
2. I was glad our teacher went with us because I feel I know my teacher better, and I think my teacher knows me better.

Put an *X* on the line of any of the following sentences that you would say about your outdoor school experience, if you could. You may mark as many sentences as you like. If you do not agree with it, put an *O* on the line.

_____ 1. It helps a person understand his school work better.
_____ 2. Most of the boys and girls cooperated in doing their share of work.
_____ 3. I think that one of the best things we learned was to take care of ourselves. We practiced habits of health by eating well-balanced meals, by getting plenty of fresh air and rest, by bathing, by brushing our teeth regularly and by getting adjusted to the setting.
_____ 4. For a long time to come I will remember how relaxed and happy I felt as I studied nature all around me.
_____ 5. I feel more grown up since the outdoor school experience.
_____ 6. I shall never forget the wonderful evenings around the campfire.
_____ 7. I learned a "whole lot" about animal life, soil, plants, and rocks.
_____ 8. After being in the forest, I realize why it is so important to practice good forest manners and conservation.
_____ 9. We learned that staying on the trail, keeping together and avoiding poison oak are some of the important safety measures taken for hiking in the forest.
_____10. Guarding our forests against fires means more to me now that I have lived in the forest.
_____11. After exploring in the outdoors, I realize that almost every creature and every plant seem to have a place and purpose.

Read each question and then mark an "X" in one of the three columns at the right.

	Yes	No	Not Sure
1. If you had another chance, would you like to go to the outdoor school?			
2. Do you feel you made some new friends there?			
3. Before you went to the outdoor school, did you have a hobby? What? _____			

	Yes	No	Not Sure
4. Did you learn anything new that you might like to continue as a hobby? What? _____ _____			
5. If a boy or girl were afraid of snakes, other creatures, or of the woods and darkness, do you think the outdoor school might help to overcome some of these fears?			
6. Did you learn to like any food you had not eaten before, or any food you usually do not eat? What? _____ _____			
7. Did you learn anything new or important about the outdoors? What? _____ _____			
8. Would you like to see some changes made in the outdoor school program? What _____ _____			
9. Did you learn anything new or important about conservation of our natural resources? What? _____ _____			
10. Since your outdoor experience, have you read any books about trees or other plants, rocks, starts, animals, water cycle, etc., for your *own* interest? What? _____ _____			

Underline *three* of the things you enjoyed most of the outdoor school.

Trip to the forest   Square dancing

Trip to the gravel pit   Nature games

Trip to the swamp   Compass games

Trip to the stream   Astronomy

Trip to the abandoned farm   Friendliness of all

Campfires   Archery

Meals   Casting and fishing

Chores   Shooting

Living with my classmates   Boating

Mail from home   Swimming

Star study   Skiing

Vesper service   Others _____

Crafts   _____

If I could go to the outdoor sc

_____   _____ .

DATE DUE

APR 2 9 2002			

Demco, Inc. 38-293